Advance praise for

From Scratch

Dennis Griffin has performed a valuable service for the Treasure Valley in telling the story of CWI's creation and serving as CWI's founding President. For those who believe in the right of the people to use local government and its power to tax to improve the lives of its citizens, *From Scratch* is a must read.

Bob Kustra*, President, Boise State University*

I have known Dennis Griffin as a superb speaker and communicator, and now know he has a rare talent for writing as well. This is one of those reads that is hard to put down: you just want to keep moving on to the next chapter; the next story. We have seen all growth records for new community colleges shattered with CWI; history is being made right before our eyes. If you want to know about the "perfect storm" that made this all possible, you must read this book.

Tom Dale*, Mayor, City of Nampa*

Dennis Griffin's exhaustively researched book is an engrossing history of the decades of frustrations and disappointments (including some until-now undisclosed behind-the-scenes struggles) that preceded realization of the dream – creation of a new community college in Idaho's largest metropolitan area. The college's virtually instant success underscores the validity of that vision.

Steve Ahrens*, former president,*
Idaho Association of Commerce & Industry

Dr. Griffin's extensive experience with Boise State University and service as the first President of the College of Western Idaho makes him the ideal person to explain the history and development of the College. This book is accurate, thorough, and the product of a person who was truly in the trenches.

Guy Hurlbutt*, member,*
College of Western Idaho Board of Trustees

(Courtesy of CWI)

FROM SCRATCH

Inside the Lightning Launch of the College of Western Idaho

Dr. Dennis E. Griffin

Founding President Emeritus

Foreword by Idaho Governor C.L. "Butch" Otter

RIDENBAUGH PRESS

Carlton, Oregon

Ridenbaugh Press

P.O. 834, Carlton OR 97111

(503) 852-0010

www.ridenbaughpress.com

contact: stapilus@ridenbaugh.com

Composition and editing by Ridenbaugh Press, Carlton, Oregon.

Cover design by Randy Stapilus.

Library of Congress Cataloging-in-Publication Data:

Griffin, Dennis

From Scratch: Inside the Lightning Launch of the College of Western Idaho

ISBN 9780945648116 (softbound)

1. United States-Northwest-education. 2. Community Colleges. 3. College of Western Idaho. I. Title.

Printed in the United States of America.

December 2011

10 9 8 7 6 5 4 3 2 1

This Book Is Dedicated To:

A Board of Trustees who committed themselves fully to create a community college: Jerry Hess, Guy Hurlbutt, Mark Dunham, Mary Carol (M.C.) Niland, Hatch Barrett, Stan Bastian, and Tammy Ray.

and

An Executive Team who worked tirelessly and no matter how crazy things got, didn't know the meaning of the word quit: Victor Watson, Cheryl Wright, Brian Currin, Shirl Boyce, Cathy Hampton, and Debbie Jensen.

and

Most importantly, my wife Joni who never let me get too discouraged, and who was my most ardent supporter during this whole adventure. I love and appreciate you so much, Joni.

“Until you have done something for humanity,
you should be ashamed to die.”

Horace Mann

“Education is more than a luxury; it is
a responsibility that society owes to itself.”

Daniel Boorstin

Table of Contents

FORWARD

By C.L. "Butch Otter"

"Opportunities may come but they never linger."

"The greatest achievement of the human spirit is to live up to one's opportunities, and make the most of one's resources."

Luc deClapiers, Marquis de Vauvenargues, 1715-1747

This book is about opportunity and those who stepped forward to help create a comprehensive community college in southwestern Idaho.

It is about the five people who stepped forward to become the first trustees, the seven people who stepped forward to become the first executive team to meet the day-to-day challenges of creating a new community college, and about the hundreds of citizens who stepped forward to collect and sign petitions to bring the question to voters.

It is about the area businesses and individuals that donated funds to inform the voters and to turn out the vote.

Perhaps most importantly, it is about those who stepped forward to approve the creation of a new Idaho community college – the College of Western Idaho (CWI).

After more than 20 years and several studies, the question of creating the first community college in southwestern Idaho was put to voters in Canyon and Ada counties on May 22,

2007. A super-majority voted to create the CWI, thus extending to thousands the opportunity of local and affordable advanced education.

Only four years later, the success of this new college is well documented, and opportunities for Idahoans young and old are increasing.

CWI's successful launch is in no small part a tribute to the experience and guidance of Dr. Dennis Griffin, the founding President of CWI. He was the calming voice of reason when times were the most difficult. Dr. Griffin quickly assembled an executive team of seasoned professionals.

Along with the Board of Trustees, these motivated individuals – working as a team with a single, lofty goal in mind – established a new and historically significant institution that will benefit Idahoans for many years.

This book recognizes those individuals who "lived up to one's opportunities" and made "the most of one's resources."

Perhaps more than anything, this book emphasizes that together our efforts can contribute to an accomplishment that is greater than the sum of its ingredients. In this case, Idaho is the better for it.

As Always – Idaho, "Esto Perpetua"

C.L. "Butch" Otter

Governor of Idaho

1 Why a college matters

Kelsey White would have described herself in high school as a rebel who lived to party. She carried a lot of baggage and little self-confidence. But a few years after high school, she decided her life "was going nowhere fast," and at age 22, she made the giant step of enrolling at the College of Western Idaho with its first academic class, at its grand opening, in January 2009.

White's teachers at CWI saw the potential in her. She joined the debate team, bolstered by the encouragement of debate coach Michelle Bennett, who kept pushing her.

"I went from 'no way' to 'maybe it's possible,' to 'maybe I'll try,' to 'let's go for it,'" she recalled. White said she owes much to Michelle, who never gave up encouraging her and believing in her even when she didn't believe in herself.

She became an integral part of the award-winning debate team and president of the History Club. She says she never would have ventured outside of herself without Michelle's urging. Professor Bennett would "sit down and talk with me and help me all the time," she recalls, and now Kelsey feels as though she has a friend for life. She credits Michelle for helping her develop her critical thinking skills.

Kelsey also gives credit to several other CWI professors who stood beside her and encouraged her. Reggie Jayne singled her out as a leader. Scott Weaver urged her to be what she really wanted to be. Johnny Rowing taught her the technical side of debate. Heather Thompson "always had time to sit down and talk to me. She had a great teaching style and made a huge difference in my life."

Kelsey White was graduated in the spring of 2011 with an AA degree in Communications. She believes that she truly felt love from these and many other teachers at CWI. As a result of this mentoring, she plans to enroll at BSU to obtain her bachelor's degree, followed by a master's and Ph.D. Her ultimate goal is to teach at a community college, preferably CWI, where she can guide young people in a manner similar to the way she was steered by her "wonderful professors."

She believes that she is beginning to realize her potential as a result of her teachers' encouragement and belief in what she could do, and expressed her gratitude for their caring guidance.

Before 2009, none of that would have happened, because before 2009, there was no College of Western Idaho.

This is the story of how that college came to be.

But first I'd like to say a few words about *why* it came to be.

Early in the process, I'd spoken to many groups around the Treasure Valley trying to drum up support for a community college as well as pushing for one after it was apparent that the referendum would take place. It is one thing to talk about these concepts in the abstract, quite another to hear the stories of real people whose lives were transformed by the creation of the college.

I stressed how these same successes would impact society in terms of the welfare and crime rolls as well as provide for an increasingly demanding workforce.

But the central theme of my presentations was always how profoundly a vibrant community college would change the lives of people who might otherwise be lost.

Over coffee Russ Keely, 50, divorced with two children, told me his story of a life given another chance by CWI.

"I have probably been an alcoholic since I took my first drink at a party when I was just 13 years old. ... Everything good in my life up until my incarceration at Cottonwood, from sports, working good jobs, and most importantly my ex-wife and children, I managed to screw up by my drinking."

He has been sober since October 2008 while incarcerated at the North Idaho Correctional Institution for DUI conviction. He now attends AA meetings on a regular basis and knows that he is just one drink away from going right back where he was – in prison.

While in prison, a counselor got him excited about going back to school. He had been enrolled at Boise State University from 1979-81, but spent most of his time there partying.

Keely enrolled at CWI, and he was graduated in May 2011. He not only credits the faculty at the new community college with helping to save his life, but also for opening doors to new opportunities that he didn't know existed. He is convinced that without the encouragement and guidance he received at CWI he would be "either in prison or a hopeless drunk."

As this is written, Keely is enrolled as a full-time student at BSU, majoring in accounting with a minor in addiction studies. He hopes to graduate in December 2012, then open his own accounting office during the day while counseling others struggling with addiction at night.

He credits his newfound success to instructors at CWI who were both "passionate about their subjects and really cared about their students as people." He named five faculty members who were especially supportive and helpful to him: Heather Thompson, John Nordstrom, Joe Welker, Reggie Jayne and Ander Sundell.

Russ was also encouraged to get involved in student government while at CWI. He was appointed to the first Student Senate where he served as student body treasurer, a position he never expected the school would allow a convicted felon to fill. "I'm grateful they trusted me," he said.

Keely also helped write the first Associated Students of the College of Western Idaho Constitution and budget. Terry Blom and Alicia Peterson (from the student services department) furnished invaluable help and support while he served on the Student Senate, he said.

Russ has maintained his interest in student government by serving on the Associated Students Funding Board when he moved on to BSU.

During my campaigning for CWI's creation I often talked about the community college's role in retraining. Sherman Kester's story is a powerful validation of my argument.

Sherman had worked 15 years for Micron as an operator, then as a production supervisor. While employed there, he attended BSU and earned his AAS in Electronics in 2005, allowing him to become a technician and build robots.

He took a voluntary layoff package in 2008 after facing the third round of personnel cuts at Micron, and took advantage of his layoff to return to school. He signed up for computer studies, feeling the need to expand his education beyond electronics and soon focused on computer security, especially information security and forensics.

Don Bowers, the CWI program director, had impressed Sherman during an orientation presentation, he said. He also heard good reports about the program and Bower's teaching from area experts in the field. Since the program was part of the Larry Selland College of Applied Technology at BSU, it was transferred to CWI during his second year. He was concerned initially that the transfer might hurt his academic standing. Sherman's fears soon faded as he grew to support the affiliation with CWI and graduated in the spring of 2010 with an AAS Degree with two certifications – networking and security, both requiring national exams.

Sherman went to work for the Canyon County Sheriff's Department in August 2010 as a media storage technician. One month after he started his new job, the IT firewall failed. He was able to help construct a temporary firewall while a new one was being purchased and the department was kept up and running.

You can only imagine the problems that might result when a law enforcement agency loses its IT security. Sherman obviously felt validated and competent as result of being able to deal with the computer problems fortified by the knowledge he had gained in the CWI program. The sheriff's department also commended his actions.

"Don Bowers taught me everything," he said. "He not only is a great teacher but he took a personal interest in me."

"Bowers went out of his way more than once to help me," Kester continued. On top of that, he pointed out that Bowers works hard to stay current in an ever-changing field and stay active with the Information Systems Security Association.

Sherman is now a member of the program's technical advisory committee.

Bryan Grasmick, 35, and single, had three strikes against him before he finished high school at a local alternative school.

He was kicked out of his regular high school for drug-use and fighting in his junior year. He got married immediately after high school, and had two children right away, but he continued using drugs, which cost him his marriage and family. Bryan was sent to prison for six years in 2006 for drug-related offenses. He said he "never felt so alone and discouraged in his life" as he did while serving his prison sentence before being paroled in 2008.

When Bryan was released in 2008, his dad recommended enrolling in the Heavy Duty Truck Technician Program at BSU. His father had previously hired a graduate of that program and felt he had been well prepared and had done a good job.

Bryan said he "was scared to death" and felt overwhelmed when he started the program in the fall of 2008. Considering his bad experiences in high school, failed marriage, and his mistakes in general, Bryan said he didn't have much confidence and "doubted that he could be successful." He feared he would fall back with his old friends and into his habits of drug use. The program director Steve Rayburn, encouraged him from the start and with that support, combined with determination and hard work, Bryan began to taste success.

Rayburn pushed him to enter a writing contest in his English composition class and he won, receiving the President's Choice Award for writing a paper entitled *Illusion of Power* that portrayed his years of drug abuse. Rayburn also made sure he entered several skills contests in which he also excelled.

Bryan's plate was full as he continued to work the program. In addition to spending six hours a day in class, he spent 10 hours a week in parole classes, many hours studying for both classes, and caring for his child each day.

Since it, too, was part of the Selland College, the truck technician program was transferred to CWI during Bryan's second year. Although the transfer came as a surprise he said the changeover went smoothly. At first he and others expressed concern "because they would not have a degree from BSU" but rather from a college they had never heard of, but their concern lessened when they realized their fees were reduced by 50 percent.

Bryan was graduated in the spring of 2010 with an AAS degree, finishing with a 3.90 GPA. He was offered a job with Northwest Equipment Company where he had interned as a student. Bryan told me he "loves his job," looks forward to moving up in the company, and says the program changed his life. He is getting married soon and said he is "the happiest he has ever been."

While he acknowledges that Rayburn was the toughest teacher he had, "he was also the best," and he owes him a lot, as well as all of his general education instructors. He also had good words for Alex Beal, another one of his teachers in the program.

Teresa Fridich, now in her early 40s, was given up for adoption at birth. Her adoptive father abused her for many years and Teresa's behavior reflected the damage such abuse does. She ended up living out her high school years in a group home, and was emancipated during her sophomore year.

Teresa moved to Boise after dropping out of Mount Hood Community College in Oregon. She worked at several jobs in the Boise area but was overcome by her personal demons in ways that are difficult to imagine: 10 years of illegal drug abuse, her biological father was murdered, a marriage fell apart; and she continues to battle cancer, and is now facing a new round of radiation therapy.

She had reached the end of her rope after being laid off from MPC in 2008, which led to a botched suicide attempt.

Two weeks later, Teresa saw an ad for the new community college starting up in the valley and decided to check it out. After visiting the CWI campus she said she felt at home from the first time she walked into the classroom building in Nampa.

"People seemed so friendly and supportive," she said; "I felt like a number during a similar visit to BSU."

Even so when she started in the first class in January 2009, she returned to the classroom with a monster chip on her shoulder. She described herself as "sarcastic, withdrawn, verbally abusive and untrusting."

But her negative attitude didn't last long, because despite her mind-set, she was met with nothing but support from the faculty. Soon she began to feel that she was "not beyond redemption."

She attributes her about-face to faculty members who made a significant difference in her life – Michael Robinson, Charles Dickinson, Andrea Ascuena and Michelle Bennett. She also expressed gratitude to Cheryl Wright, Ellen Spencer, and Jennifer Hedges (staff members) who "saw something within me that was worth salvaging. I owe them everything."

Starting as a young woman with no confidence, Teresa tried out for the new debate team, eventually becoming captain and winning several awards. In the process of overcoming her laundry list of problems, she developed a heart for giving back.

She is passionate about volunteering to clean the garbage out of canals and drain ditches in the Nampa area and was named volunteer of the year for the Idaho Wildlife Federation – she is often referred to as the Angel of Wilson Creek which feeds the fish hatchery and fishing ponds on the grounds at the Regional Idaho Fish and Game Office in Nampa.

Teresa said she "came to CWI for an education, but found a life," noting that the caring supportive people at CWI literally saved her life. After graduating from CWI in May 2009, she was awarded a scholarship to the College of Idaho in Caldwell. She currently works full time for CWI and hopes to continue her employment there while she completes her bachelor's degree.

I will forever be moved by these students' stories and the way they took control of their lives. The one common theme was the way their instructors took a personal interest in them and motivated them to be successful even though they didn't think they could be. As I listened, I thought back to my own philosophy of the importance of students having kind, caring teachers who support and encourage them, helping them develop the confidence to succeed.

For too long, southwestern Idaho's Treasure Valley was the largest metropolitan area in the nation without a comprehensive community college. Thousands of students like Kelsey, Russ, Sherman, Bryan, and Teresa were underserved or not served at all. On another level, Idaho's businesses were not getting enough trained employees, and the valley was routinely bypassed by companies seeking to expand – an important issue in a time of economic troubles.

Hope finally arrived when the citizens of Ada and Canyon counties voted in 2007 to create a community college district and most importantly agreed to tax themselves in order to do it. Given the severe downturn of the economy this event seemed surprising, but at the same time reaffirmed that the citizens of both counties fully understood the overwhelming need for a community college and the impact it would make on people's lives and drive the economy.

I had the honor of serving as the founding president for the first two years of CWI's operation. We started from scratch—we didn't even exist as a legal entity—growing to a full, comprehensive community college serving more than 3,600 credit/transfer students and in excess of 12,000 non-credit students in seven locations throughout the two counties within two years.

Those two years were filled with long hours and hard work shouldered by the finest group of people with whom I have ever worked. That group included our Board of Trustees and six dedicated professionals who comprised my Executive Team. Over the two years my team spent an incredible amount of time together working through many challenges, most of which we couldn't possibly have predicted.

We all will look back in a few years and be thankful that we were given the opportunity to be part of this historic undertaking. We all felt honored to be a part of it.

What follows are my personal reflections, starting with how I became the unlikely first president of the College of Western Idaho and how, within two years, this fledgling community college was conceived and positioned for unprecedented growth.

2 Opportunity of a Lifetime

The first CWI Board of Trustees was sworn in on July 30, 2007. They met in my building at the West Campus of Boise State University in Nampa where I worked as Executive Director of BSU West. Milford Terrell, State Board of Education President, swore in the new trustees. The mood was upbeat and hopeful. They then went into executive session, excusing everyone, including me. I was told later that their first priority was to select a president and do it quickly because they knew there was a multitude of challenges ahead, and they needed the expertise of a professional educator, an administrator. They had to choose the best approach to move forward and had to do so rapidly—my phone rang less than a week later.

The board had chosen Jerry Hess, a Nampa entrepreneur and longtime education advocate, to be their first chairman. Jerry always called me the day before each meeting, which happened several times during that short week, to secure a meeting room. I got wind that the trustees were considering me as president, but I knew I would be a long shot given my lack of experience working directly in a community college setting.

I'll never forget that day: August 6, 2007, when Jerry called again making sure that the room was ready for the board meeting scheduled at 9:00 the next morning.

"Oh, by the way, I expect you to submit a resume tomorrow," he said casually. I asked why I should, and he said, "To be interviewed for president." I told him I didn't have a current resume because I hadn't looked for a job in 18 years. "Get one together, expect to be interviewed and be prepared to tell us how you would put a community college together," he replied. He spoke casually and matter-of-factly, and offered no other information.

In fact, his comment stopped me dead in my tracks on that Monday afternoon at 3 p.m., for two very big reasons.

First, I was not the boilerplate kind of choice for running a college (or a university).

I did have the advantage of being highly familiar with the project. For months, I had been heavily involved in the effort to create a new community college. And for most of my adult life, I've been an administrator in higher education, at the time at Boise State University.

But most college and university presidents follow a standard career path, rising through institution-wide career steps, usually becoming an institution vice president before moving into the top job. My career path had been quite different; its trajectory didn't seem headed toward presidency of an institution. I hadn't much thought of my own professional activities in those terms.

Not only that, I had never before worked, in any capacity, for a community college.

Secondly, I was being asked to do something I had never done before—and that few people, ever, have had to do in quite this way.

The realization struck me that by 9 the next morning I had to present a resume to this new board of trustees and lay out a "simple" blueprint to initiate a college. Obviously—and this is an understatement—this was something I had never done before.

Just how *do* you create a college from scratch?

Between 3 p.m. on Monday and 9 a.m. on Tuesday I did a lot of scrambling. Sleep was not on my agenda.

To cobble together a resume, or *curriculum vitae*, I simply stole liberally from the bio I had often used as a speaking introduction, expanding on it. I spent most of every waking hour of the next 18 formulating the steps I thought should be employed to create a community college where none had existed before. I was groping around in a grey and cloudy area, new ground, never cultivated under my direction, anyway.

When 9 a.m. arrived, I put it on the line.

At my interview, the first question was: "Why do you want to be president of the college?"

I replied that I wasn't sure I *did* want to be president, given the enormity of the task ahead. And not only that, I was a short-timer, scheduled for retirement in 2009 and I had no intention of putting it off—which got a laugh. That remark was followed by various board members quipping that they weren't sure they wanted to be trustees either, what with all the work that lay ahead.

The atmosphere turned more serious as we began to debate for the next two hours.

After that, the new trustees met in executive session for about an hour. Then the door opened, they called me back in and offered me the job.

All of them were upbeat and supportive, assuring me they would be highly involved as we faced this gargantuan challenge together. Jerry Hess said that I should "look westward as I started making decisions and hiring people." One of the board members also offered advice by saying, "Don't let the grass grow under your feet."

I took the first statement to mean I should stop thinking of myself as a Boise State University employee—which I still was at that point—and start separating myself from the university. I took the second comment to mean that I needed to get this college up and running as fast as possible.

I little grasped that both issues would be among my biggest challenges.

I was, of course, elated with the appointment and could hardly believe I had been given such an amazing opportunity. Having been immersed in higher education administration since the late seventies, to now have the chance to cap my career by establishing a community college was mind-boggling. They hadn't even interviewed anyone else!

The euphoria was short-lived.

Immediately after the trustees meeting, I had an interview with Bill Roberts of the *Idaho Statesman*, received some congratulations from my colleagues, and went back to my office. Reality slapped me in the face as soon as I started thinking about the huge responsibility. What do I do first? How do I get started?

The questions came from outside as well. Starting with the ease of getting the appointment. In an *Idaho Statesman* editorial on August 9, 2007, Kevin Richert said "the process leaves us a bit troubled…they only interviewed Griffin…they may have snagged a winner, but they could have cast a wider net."

I guess I was in the right place at the right time. I was given a two-year contract and the title of Interim President; the "interim" label was soon dropped.

After returning to my office, I closed the door, sat down, kicked my feet up and began to think. Even though I was as excited as I have ever been, my immediate reaction was to experience a sinking feeling, perhaps a bit like drowning, definitely a state of being overwhelmed. I reflected on my life and how incredibly fortunate I was.

I also reflected upon how I had gotten here, given that I started life as a reluctant student, and the many stumbling blocks I encountered along the way. Some of them were the same kind of stumbling blocks many of the students to this new college would be living through.

I began to muse about my childhood in the 1940s and what I had learned along the way.

I was raised on a Payette County cattle ranch in a small three-room house complete with (until early grade school) an outhouse for a bathroom. My dad worked on the ranch, and I loved that life. My first paying job, at age eight, was driving tractor; I remember clearly how proud I was of myself. Other jobs would follow, of course, but that first one remains special. And there were always daily chores my brother and I were required to perform. I learned early from my parents the value of hard work and that I owed my employer his money's worth no matter how daunting the task seemed at the outset.

I also reflected on the 1950s, the decade and more when I attended all 12 years of public schools in Payette. I remember with a twinge of regret that because of my extreme shyness and lack of preparation for the first day of school, the first and second grades were so traumatic for me that to this day I can remember only bits and pieces of those two years. My mother had to tutor me because I fell so far behind, and she tells me that I didn't know my alphabet until the end of the second grade.

I'll always remember my fourth grade teacher, Helen Cheek, the first teacher who took a personal interest in me—she helped me catch up with the rest of the students.

We moved to town just before I started the seventh grade where slowly during junior high and high school, I began to enjoy school, and as a result my new-found confidence began to grow. I ventured into sports, student government, music, and debate. Many teachers made a difference in my life, but the two who stood out were Dale Corn and Ellsworth Haas because they took a special interest and mentored me. They impacted my life, and other teachers began to break through my protective shell of shyness as my interest in education grew; a career path, at least subconsciously, began to take shape. I learned that one caring teacher can make a difference in the life of any successful adult.

I thought about how unlikely it was to be named a college president given my childhood as a shy little kid who struggled in school and with no support or encouragement from my parents to advance beyond high school.

This concept of lack of formal educational construct seemed understandable—it was just never discussed. My dad, a hard-working man, was unable to finish high school. He had to work to help support his family. My mother completed high school and even tried one semester of college but dropped out because she, too, was needed on the family farm.

My maternal grandfather, who I greatly admired and spent many childhood hours with, only finished the fourth grade. He had a profound influence on my life—he was wise and kind, and definitely hard-working. He reflected much wisdom. I remember as a youngster, our many trips to town together, his introducing me to everyone with such pride and how good that made me feel.

After moving into town from the farm, he managed a cemetery where I worked in the summers. A memory of him that still brings a smile to my face—my granddad digging graves by hand and singing to me. He loved the railroad and taught me all the lyrics to the old railroad song, "Casey Jones."

He also would sprinkle in a few words of advice, now and then, intermingled with the songs.

"Den," he would say, "You can never go wrong being honest and working hard."

He taught me how to work with my hands. I learned skills and developed dexterity that I find useful to this day. He taught me patience as he showed me firsthand the value of completing a job once you have begun.

I learned how important the lessons are that adults can model for youth such as honesty, kindness, patience, and mentoring just by being there for kids. I learned from him to accept others and not to judge people by society's standards (education attainment, economic status, etc.) and that one can find dignity in work no matter what that work is. As I grew into my teens, I was expected to have a job in the summertime and earn enough money to buy my school clothes and have some spending money for the school year.

I began to love learning for the first time in high school, though you wouldn't know it by my grades. I instinctively knew, also, that it was up to me to figure out what I wanted to pursue as a career and to find a way to accomplish those goals. But I also knew my parents would support my decisions in whatever way they could.

I was graduated from high school in the early 1960s, having already joined the Army National Guard. After that, I took classes for a year and a half at Boise Junior College (as the current Boise State University was then called). I got married, had two children, and started a career in banking while completing Officer Candidate School in the Army. Then I returned to Boise State College to complete my degree.

I crammed a lot into that decade as I struggled to find direction and identity.

While I enjoyed learning, I didn't last at BJC. I wasn't ready to apply myself academically, nor was I motivated to study. I quit school and went to work for a bank. Ironically, my motivation to study began to grow while I was there. My first successful classroom experience involved taking courses through the bank, and that whetted my appetite for more. On top of that, I was training new college graduates who were in the bank management training program and who earned twice what I did. A college education became more and more attractive, so finally I decided to return and finish my degree.

By this time I had complicating factors. When I once more matriculated to Boise State College, I had a wife and two children to support (I never seem to do anything the easy way). I also faced one old familiar challenge—lack of academic preparation—that I had in junior college. On top of that, I was still in the Guard attending regular drills, working two part-time jobs and had borrowed a significant amount in student loans.

Initially I planned to major in business and return to banking after graduation, but the National Guard changed all that. I was asked to teach some classes, which is typical after a person reaches a certain level of training in the Guard, and if they are capable. Even though I didn't want to teach at first, I acquiesced and then to my surprise grew to love it. I began to realize that I had discovered my purpose in life.

I changed my college major from business to education, graduating in three years to become a teacher. I learned another important lesson regarding perseverance: There is a payoff if you just hang in there and see things through no matter how difficult they become.

During the 1970s, I started my first teaching job at Nampa High School followed by my second at Capital High School. I was able to complete my master's degree in three and a half years. The decade also had personal setbacks, in the form of a painful divorce.

The irony of me becoming an educator was evident as I reflected back on my early life and failures as a student. I have always wondered if all the academic and maturity challenges motivated me to teach and help kids who struggled as I did.

Because of the experiences and lessons I had learned along the way, I wanted to help those troubled students—in fact that became my cause. I focused on students who were not well liked by other kids, or who had personal issues that prevented them from being part of the in-crowd or any crowd. I remember serving on a number of scholarship committees over the years, and I would always fight for the kids who perhaps weren't the best students academically, but who had the greatest need and potential. I worked hard to be the best teacher I could be.

I believed that too much emphasis was placed on getting a college degree and vocational technical education was judged as a second-class pursuit. I knew that most of the high school students I worked with would not complete a four-year degree and I worked to help them understand that there is value in learning and training in whatever form it takes. I tried to teach them that satisfaction in their chosen career was far more important than what anyone else thought. I tried to help them understand that pursuing a career had little to do with how much money they could earn and had a lot to do with whether or not they had a passion for their work. I preached constantly that, "If you love what you are doing, the money will follow."

During the 1980s, I grew restless and even though I had enjoyed high school teaching, I felt I needed a new challenge. I answered an ad in the paper, interviewed and was offered a position that resulted in my becoming the Director of Education of ITT Links School of Business in Boise (a private post-secondary vocational technical school). That led to a transfer to Seattle as an ITT School Director. After I was there a couple of years, I was pursued by another company. In taking that job, I became president and CEO of a five-campus school operation.

I realized after nine years, living there and doing that kind of work, I missed public education and the Treasure Valley. I would often say that if I could wave a magic wand, I would move back to Boise and work at Boise State University which by then had evolved into a young and vibrant urban institution.

By then remarriage and a step-daughter also had come into my life. Finally after my career soul-searching continued unabated for a time, following discussions with my wife, I asked Joni to take a leap of faith and move back to Boise. With her support, I resigned and we packed up and left for Idaho. When we came back, in 1988, we arrived without a job between us, and we lived in my brother's basement for several months until we both had landed jobs. That was certainly a humbling experience after the position I had held just prior in Seattle, but in retrospect good for the soul.

The 1990s opened exciting new ventures in a career with Boise State, the smartest move I ever made professionally (even though it also meant a 60 percent cut in pay initially). I'll always be grateful for the help Larry Selland, BSU's Vice President for Academic Affairs, gave me in getting the position with BSU. I also earned my doctorate, in the fall of 1996, after studying evenings and attending summer schools for 5½ years. I did my doctoral dissertation on conducting a survey of Idaho high school counselors to gage their attitudes and knowledge of post-secondary vocational technical education. While working for BSU I retired from the Army Reserve after 32 years of service.

What is interesting is that with every change I made, there were people who questioned my sanity for taking such risks, saying that I should play it safe and stay the course. All of this was valuable experience as I later counseled others.

Now I had the opportunity to complete my career not only as a college president, but as the first president of a new institution that I would be helping to create; especially an institution that catered to many of the students I had always been drawn to helping. This was more than I could have ever asked for.

I thought about all the obstacles I faced at CWI because we really were starting with absolutely nothing—no facilities, no money, no faculty or staff, no accreditation, no infrastructure of any kind; in fact we didn't even exist as a business or legal entity. I thought about the environment in which I would be operating. I would be under a constant spotlight with high expectations by many in the community as well as the trustees —I wondered if I could handle the stress at my age. I reflected on the issue of working for a board of trustees—in effect I would have five bosses all with their own challenges of getting a handle on their jobs while learning to work together. For many years I had enjoyed the luxury of working relatively autonomously with no daily supervision.

Was I the right person to launch a college?

Not long ago, individual board members I talked with shared their reasons for choosing me given my lack of experience working directly in a community college.

They gave several reasons for why they hired me. I did have experience as president/CEO of a chain of private vocational-technical schools in the Seattle area during the 1980s. I then worked for Boise State for 18 years, first as a Division Manager for the Larry G. Selland College of Applied Technology, then as Executive Director of BSU West. I was stationed in Canyon County during those 18 years. While serving as the Executive Director of BSU West, I reported to the Provost and worked with the President of BSU.

We were already operating, in essence, a community college in Canyon County as a part of the university. BSU was first established as a junior college in 1932 and evolved into a four-year institution in 1967, but it retained the junior college mission for Region III of Idaho until the emergence of CWI.

BSU West offered most of the first two years' general subjects (core classes) for the BA/BS degrees. In addition, we included a variety of credit driven professional-technical programs as well as adult basic education and workforce training.

The Boise State students who attended BSU West liked it because they interacted in a more intimate setting, mostly with teachers who only wanted to teach (as opposed to conducting research, establishing rank, tenure, etc.). They experienced what was in many ways a community college without the label. It was a sizable operation, numbering about 3,000 academic credit/transfer students, six professional technical programs with approximately 250 students as well as about 6,000 non-credit students in either adult basic education or workforce training.

So why wouldn't BSU West continue to serve the Treasure Valley as well as a community college would?

The major problem was that the academic credit/transfer students had to meet the admissions requirements of BSU, the highest for a state school in Idaho, while paying full university fees. In addition, they were part of the university culture which generally isn't as supportive and nurturing for struggling students as a community college is.

The professional-technical students, although experiencing open admissions, still had to pay full university fees which were considerably higher than the two existing Idaho community colleges. Since the hallmark of any community college is access and affordability, it was difficult for many students to participate.

BSU's Canyon County Center began in a partially remodeled lumber retail building in the mid 60s. When I arrived in 1989, only a few academic, vocational technical and adult basic classes were offered. It steadily grew with support from the main campus. I served as the facilities manager, oversaw the programs, made recommendations for new programs, and spent a lot of time on community and public relations.

I had been actively involved in the community for 18 years. I served on the board of directors for the Nampa Chamber of Commerce and in 1998-99 was elected chairman. I was a member of the Nampa Rotary Club serving on the board as well as being named president in 1992-93. I served on numerous other boards, including the Caldwell Chamber of Commerce, Idaho State School and Hospital, and the United Way of Canyon County, in addition to the Idaho Center Advisory Board, the Nampa Visions Committee, and the Idaho Lifelong Learning Association.

My point is—the newly appointed CWI Board of Trustees saw me as someone who had the breadth of educational management experience they were looking for along with involvement in and respect of the community at large. Another factor was that to be realistic, the board didn't have the luxury of time. If the trustees had gone out to conduct a national search, they would have needed several months to get a president on board. If that new president was required to conduct a national search to hire an executive team, another months' long delay would have ensued. It is probable that a team would not have been in place for six to eight months at the earliest, and the board members were already feeling pressure from citizens to get the college up and running.

Another key ingredient was the fact that the trustees clearly understood there would have to be a connection to BSU for a period of time, including the major hurdle of transferring the Selland College of Applied Technology from BSU to CWI. This "un-entangling" of the Selland College from BSU and the State of Idaho, presented major challenges that would prove to be one of the major stumbling blocks over the entire first two years. They saw me as someone with experience in that arena who could help navigate the turbulent waters.

It took courage on the part of the board of trustees to choose me to lead this start-up operation while taking some flak for it.

3 Decades of Discussion

The origins of Idaho's community college world trace back to Boise in 1932, when the Episcopal Church founded (on church property) a small women's college, Boise College, later Boise Junior College. When, after a couple of years, church funding was stretched and closure was imminent, the Boise Chamber of Commerce, which very much wanted a college of some kind in Boise, offered to keep it going. After a few years of operation by a committee of the chamber, members decided it should be a public college, and pushed a bill through the Idaho Legislature allowing local regions to set up junior college taxing districts. The Boise area in 1939 set up the first, operating Boise Junior College, which later that year moved to its current location in the middle of the city on the Boise River on the old Boise Airport site.

After the conversion in 1965 of BJC to Boise College, Idaho had only two comprehensive community colleges—North Idaho College, created in 1933 in Coeur d'Alene, and the College of Southern Idaho, established in 1965 in Twin Falls. In addition, professional-technical programs were available through Eastern Idaho Technical College in Idaho Falls. Throughout the rest of the state, the community college mission was delivered within three other four-year institutions—Boise State University, Idaho State University in Pocatello and Lewis Clark State College in Lewiston.

Over the past four decades, numerous discussions by the state legislature and various task forces centered on the idea of expanding community colleges in Idaho. Such discussions usually dealt with formation of a community college system and/or a clarification of the roles of the state college and the two state universities' delivery of community college courses and programs.

Of all of Idaho's professional organizations, the one most deeply involved with reforming higher education was the Idaho Association of Commerce and Industry (IACI). For nearly four decades IACI has been one of the most influential groups of business leaders in the state. IACI worked diligently lobbying the legislature to reform higher education, beginning in the 1970s and continuing to the present. A leading proponent of expanding Idaho's community college offerings was Steve Ahrens, who in nearly nine years as a lobbyist for Boise Cascade Corporation and 15 years as president of IACI, had worked with the public and the Idaho Legislature to create a new community college in Southwest Idaho.

Ahrens recalled that IACI's involvement began at a summer meeting in McCall in 1981. (My thanks to Steve for both his written and oral history on IACI's involvement.) Chuck Jepson of Hewlett-Packard delivered a report that included, among other things, data indicating his company was having difficulty finding qualified graduates on Idaho's campuses.

Two months later the IACI Board met and John Clute proposed that the members of IACI conduct a study of Idaho's higher education system. The board approved, authorizing Bob Moss to appoint an ad hoc committee to put together a proposal. John Clute (general counsel, Boise Cascade Corporation) chaired the committee with members L.N. (Bud) Purdy (Picabo Livestock Company), Ray Smelek (Hewlett-Packard, Company), John Forbes (Tupperware Company) and Ed Osborne (Ore-Ida Foods, Inc.).

This committee fundamentally changed the direction of IACI, which up to then had dealt only with business issues. Idaho's business community supported the education development effort in a major way, with corporate jets crisscrossing the state, carrying high-priced executives who volunteered countless hours and personal time for the study. Public information meetings were held in all parts of the state to hear testimony and to explain the committee's findings. They even raised nearly $200,000 for the study.

The one person integral to all that IACI did in those days was Pat K. Harwood, who served as IACI president from 1976-1986. Steve says that Pat did more individually to create the kind of organization IACI became than any other individual.

In 1983, IACI published the study, called *Higher Education in Idaho: A Plan for the Future.*

It was presented during the 1984 legislative session, and the legislators spent considerable time discussing it. The report focused on faculty, facilities, governance, tuition, admission standards, institutional roles and missions, and funding. Under the area of roles and missions, the task force recommended:

■ The role and mission statement of each college and university be clarified to specify the purpose of each institution and to identify what it can and cannot do

■ A statewide community college system be organized

■ None of the universities serve as community colleges

■ New community colleges be created over the next decade or so in the Boise/Nampa/Caldwell, Pocatello, and Idaho Falls regions

■ Lewis Clark State College should serve as the community college for its region

■ All community colleges be governed by locally elected boards, coordinated by the state

■ All postsecondary vocational education preparatory and upgrading/retraining programs be delivered through the community college system, as traditionally funded, and with the state coordinating programs

■ Local financial support for each community college be provided by all its community college districts on an equitable basis

Unfortunately, despite considerable interest on the part of the legislators, little came out of IACI's efforts. Republicans, while enthusiastic about the recommendations, wanted to implement them with little or no expense. Democrats, who were eager to see the changes suggested, wanted to do so by simply spending more money with no structural change.

As so often happened historically with this issue, things screeched to a stalemate. The report did lead to the creation of the first role and mission statements for Idaho's colleges and universities, but the legislature failed to endorse the rest of the report's recommendations.

Many other studies followed:

■ a study by a Governor's Task Force on Education for the 80's

■ a study conducted by a Task Force on Vocational Education for Southwest Idaho in 1984

■ a study by the Legislative Budget Office on Junior Colleges in Idaho in 1985

■ a committee was created on Postsecondary Education in Southwest Idaho in 1989

■ a Legislative Council Committee on Community Colleges created in 1990

■ a National Center for Higher Education report was written in 1995

■ a national summary called the State Governance and Community Colleges was written in 1998

■ a Community College Development Subcommittee was established in 1998

The list goes on and on. Wheels spun in place year after year.

The arrival of Dr. Bob Kustra, named president of Boise State University in 2003, finally brought the issue to a head.

Bob Kustra is a riveting speaker with a commanding voice and great stage presence. He is convincing; in fact I have never heard anyone better at captivating an audience. His background as a former lieutenant governor and a longtime legislator in Illinois served him well in understanding and working around the power brokers of Idaho politics. He spent much time and political capital with the legislature and with the public pushing a community college in the Treasure Valley. I think I can fairly say that CWI would not exist without the persistent and effective message he so convincingly pushed over a long period of time.

He quickly organized a campaign to convince the citizens of Treasure Valley and Idaho legislators that there needed to be a true comprehensive community college here, and that BSU's responsibility for the delivery of professional-technical programs via the Selland College should be transferred to the community college. He also emphasized that the associate degree academic programs be transferred.

This was part of a bigger picture. Dr. Kustra dreamed of maturing BSU into a research institution, and in fact created a motto for BSU to become a "metropolitan research university of distinction." Obviously post-doctoral research didn't mesh well with the professional technical training that is such an important part of a comprehensive community college.

The reality was that BSU had become the state's largest and fastest growing university and it needed to focus on its academic, research, graduate, and post graduate mission. A community college mission simply no longer fit into the role of academic institution into which BSU was evolving.

As BSU's representative in the western part of the valley, I beat a similar drum working with leaders and speaking frequently at various civic and service club meetings.

In doing that, I was fulfilling my role as Dr. Kustra's lieutenant, pushing for the community college. But I had no reluctance in doing it. I too had long believed in the need for a community college in the Treasure Valley. Through the years I'd seen too many people who weren't ready to do university work or who couldn't afford to complete their education bump up against the walls of a university structure, and I knew that a true comprehensive community college would change their lives. I had known for some time, also, that there was a crying need for trained workers for our employers. So this opportunity to support Dr. Kustra in his dream couldn't have happened at a better time. I was fortunate to be part of the whole effort.

As I spoke to various groups, the reaction was always very positive and supportive. Only a relative few voiced concerns about how it was going to be funded. Some even said that they weren't going to pay any more taxes no matter how good it was. But these voices were in a small minority.

With so many people now advocating for a comprehensive community college for Treasure Valley, the public's interest and involvement picked up in 2005. Several community groups stepped forward. One of the most vocal was the Idaho Business Coalition for Education Excellence, an alliance of more than 80 current and former CEOs from across Idaho.

Two individuals who wrote guest opinion pieces regularly in both the *Idaho Statesman* and the *Idaho Press-Tribune* were Gary Michael, retired chairman and CEO of Albertson's, and Kevin Learned, president and CEO of The Network Group and former president of what was then called Albertson College of Idaho (now, once again, the College of Idaho). Their articles were informative and persuasive. For the *Idaho Statesman* of September 5, 2005, they co-wrote a guest opinion piece which said, "The development of an efficient, comprehensive, affordable, and accessible community college network is a key strategy that must be pursued if Idaho is to meet current and future workforce needs."

By the following year, the push became more regionalized. They wrote on August 18, 2006 that "there may not be one solution for the entire state… that the object is to provide educational access to more of our citizens at lower prices and responsiveness to the training needs of Idaho businesses, not one unified system."

Another organization that stepped up in a major way was the J.A. and Kathryn Albertson Foundation. The foundation was established in 1966 as a way to "help open doors of opportunity for others." It focused on education in Idaho and has given more than $330 million to school districts throughout the state.

So it was no surprise when, in March 2006, they offered $15 million to partner with an institution to get a community college started in Treasure Valley. They had two caveats: 1) "a legislative insurance policy in the form of a sustainable funding model, and 2) that the college would be a stand-alone, comprehensive community college within a few years." They asked for proposals from Boise State University and Treasure Valley Community College in Ontario, Oregon. The College of Southern Idaho in Twin Falls also stood ready to offer classes and made it known to the Idaho State Board of Education. Joe Scott, chairman of the Albertson Foundation, made it clear that he didn't particularly care who ultimately started the community college—"it could be a public educational institution, a consortium of corporations, or a for-profit entity in or outside of Idaho." It just had to achieve sustained funding and be independent.

While the educational institutions were formulating proposals, the 2006 Idaho Legislature wrestled with the issue. Former Governor Dirk Kempthorne proposed that the state pay for a new statewide community college system with $5 million from property taxes while using existing public buildings to save the cost of creating new campuses. That $5 million would be supplemented by money from public and private institutions.

During that session of the legislature, Senator John Goedde of Coeur d'Alene and Representative Ann Rydalch of Idaho Falls agreed on a plan that would establish a statewide community college system. It called for including new programs through Boise State University, Lewis and Clark State College, Idaho State University, and Eastern Idaho Technical College. The four-year institutions would apply to the State Board of Education for permission to begin community colleges and would split the $5 million for startup costs. It would also be paid for by 4.25 percent of overall state sales tax revenues. In addition, the new community colleges would be supported by general funds, the county liquor tax, property taxes and grants.

The Legislature failed to pass the proposal. The two issues that would come up again and again for the legislators were cost—how would they pay for an ongoing community college system, plus local control—how the local boards of trustees in the two existing community college districts would fit into the management structure of such a system.

So again we were no further ahead except for enhanced awareness of the need. The legislature did, however, set up an interim committee that held statewide hearings during the summer of 2006 to gather public input. It was co-chaired by Senator John Goedde of Coeur d'Alene and Representative Darrell Boltz of Caldwell along with 15 other legislators.

The other relevant legislative issue that year was an attempt to reduce the super majority requirement from 66 2/3 percent to 60 percent to pass special ballot measures such as this one. That issue died in the House Revenue and Taxation Committee.

Dissatisfaction spread among a growing number of people supporting a comprehensive community college in Treasure Valley. Joe Scott wrote a guest opinion piece for the *Idaho Statesman,* on April, 23, 2006, in which he pointed out that the need was already well documented in no fewer than seven studies in the last 22 years. He went on to say that "when the gavel dropped, the Legislature had referred the community college issue to an interim subcommittee...by studying this issue one more time and losing the foundation's $15 million, it was the students who were left holding the bag of lemons."

During the ongoing debate, Dr. Kustra and his management team decided to propose starting a community college as a separate college within the university and designate the west campus as the location.

Dr. Sona Andrews took the lead on the project and formed a committee to write the funding proposal. It was presented to the J.A. and Kathryn Albertson Foundation in January 2007. I served on the committee to write it and we harbored high hopes that it would be approved. Our thinking was based on the concept that if BSU could get a community college up and running, the university would eventually spin it off to become a separate entity.

However, the foundation rejected the proposal for around $71 million. We were told to reduce the scope and resubmit. We did and again it was rejected. The give and take continued for some time. While this discussion continued, several committees were formed at BSU to organize an operational plan to actually staff and manage a community college should the funding materialize.

Subsequent rounds of negotiations between BSU and the Albertson Foundation seemed to go on and on. Since that process only ended in stalemate, it was obvious that another approach was necessary.

The biggest problem? Conventional wisdom held that tax-shy voters would never approve taxing themselves to create a community college district, especially given the economic climate. Dr. Kustra and I talked about the need for a strong community group to lead the charge to lobby the legislature.

At that time, in early 2007, I served on the Nampa Chamber of Commerce Executive Board. After one of our meetings, I sat down with Chairman of the Board M.C. Niland and Chamber President Georgia Bowman and talked with them about stepping up to the task of carrying the water to the legislature. M.C. said that they would and, in addition, proposed that supporters go ahead and submit the issue as a referendum. It seemed at the time to be a long shot, but at that point we thought, why not? After all, nothing ventured, nothing gained.

I must heap credit on M.C. Niland who in addition to her chamber duties, served as the President and CEO of Western Idaho Training Company (WITCO). WITCO is a sheltered workshop which trains hundreds of developmentally disabled people with skills so that they can feel useful and in many cases work in society. She had been a long-time advocate for others and working to establish a community college fit perfectly into her belief system.

The Nampa Chamber drafted a petition and obtained the required signatures to place the measure on the ballot. After that, the issue took on a life of its own. Soon the Boise Metro Chamber of Commerce, along with the chambers of Meridian and Eagle, were on board as well as civic and service organizations across the valley. Business and political leaders also added their support.

In January 2007, in his State of the State address to the legislature, Governor Butch Otter proposed providing $5 million seed money to any area of the state that would vote to form a community college district; the legislature approved it. In addition, the "Community College Yes Committee" was formed to raise the considerable amount of money needed to get the issue passed when it was placed before the voters.

Throughout all of this interaction, the importance of the J.A. and Kathryn Albertson Foundation cannot be overstated. They spent an incredible amount of money and put on a community awareness campaign called "Community College Now," which was instrumental in helping people understand from the very beginning what a community college is, what it does, and how crucial it was for the Treasure Valley to embrace having its own institution.

4 The Campaign

For those who believe in providence or destiny, what happened in the Treasure Valley to propel CWI from a dream into reality would confirm those beliefs. Some would describe it as "the stars being perfectly aligned."

Whatever you choose to call it, magic happened.

As was previously mentioned, in early 2004, Boise State President Kustra began to speak often to community leaders about the need for a community college here in the valley, and I was conducting a similar supporting campaign in my role representing BSU in western Treasure Valley.

A key player, also discussed, was the J.A. and Kathryn Albertson Foundation (JKAF). The foundation, in July 2004, set out to explore ways to start a community college in Treasure Valley and spent the rest of that year and much of the next researching and investigating community colleges. In June 2005, they received their first proposal from BSU to start a community college. By October of that year, BSU had submitted several versions of the original blueprint. JKAF also asked Treasure Valley Community College (TVCC) in Ontario, OR to submit a plan, which they did in January 2006. In March JKAF offered the Idaho State Board of Education $15 million to start a community college.

That June Lori Fisher, Executive Director of JKAF, testified regarding the urgent need for a comprehensive community college before a legislative committee. During the rest of the summer foundation leadership also met with the Idaho Business Coalition for Excellence in Education (IBCEE), the Idaho Association of Commerce and Industry (IACI), the Boise Metro Chamber of Commerce, various county and city associations, and other community organizations.

JKAF had heard for too long how employers were forced to look outside Idaho for skilled workers, so between 2004-2007, they ran a Community College Initiative in search of a solution. As part of this initiative, a public information program called "Community College Now" played pervasively in the media providing an informational web site, brochures, and public information pieces on local radio, television, and newspapers, building awareness by Treasure Valley citizens of the need. It was a brilliant campaign.

The foundation hired Scott Peyron and Associates to handle the publicity, and much of the credit goes to Stephanie Worrell who spearheaded the project. Stephanie subsequently left Peyron and started her own company, Red Sky Public Relations, and we hired her to do our first marketing campaign and other projects. She exhibited exceptional knowledge concerning community colleges, and working with her allowed us to continue with the informative campaign JKAF had initiated.

Another groundbreaking event involving JKAF was a seminal breakfast meeting in December 2006 attended by executives from the Micron Corporation and the Micron Foundation. Business and civic leaders throughout the community also heard the JKAF proposal; participants were exposed to a "short-course" on the need for a community college. JKAF did a superb job of describing the history of the community college effort in Idaho as well as the legal issues generated by the start-up of a new institution. A multitude of statistics was shared about community colleges nationally and their impact on peoples' lives and the communities in which they live from an economic development standpoint.

Dr. Kustra also raised the level of public interest, and with his efforts added to the ongoing discussion by the legislature and Governor Otter, the issue finally reached critical mass.

Another key component of this "magical happening" was the role played by the Micron Corporation. The *Idaho-Press Tribune* reported on February 23, 2007 that, "Micron is lending its political muscle, along with a promise to help pay for a college's brick and mortar in an effort to establish a community college district in Ada and Canyon counties."

Micron directed Mike Reynoldson, their Idaho Government Affairs Manager, to research the issue, and they agreed to lend the high-tech firm's wholehearted support. Mike commissioned Moore Information to do a survey. He had hired this firm before, had a high degree of confidence in their work, and knew the results would be reliable. In summary, the survey showed that 71 percent of the residents of Ada and Canyon counties wanted to see a new community college created. Sixty-five percent also believed the funding should come from a combination of state and local sources. The survey asked how much in additional property taxes homeowners would be willing to pay with the highest percentage (61%) agreeing to a figure around $12-$13 per $100,000 of their assessed property value. That dollar amount would take on a life of its own becoming a rallying point in convincing homeowners that the tax hit would be fairly painless.

As an aside...after our Board of Trustees was seated, the members felt obligated to stay with the $12-$13 "promise" made during the campaign. I fully understood that they were compelled to do that, because they viewed anything else as a "bait and switch" tactic to the people who voted to start the college. I argued that they ought to set the levy amount a little higher, because I felt we would be inundated with students and such a small amount would really hamstring us in terms of serving these freshman adequately.

The Board of Trustees stuck to their guns and the amount for the first budget cycle actually came in at $11.24. The real problem is that according to Idaho Code, public entities can raise their budget requests to the counties each year by no more than three percent per year plus new construction and by setting the rate so low, we would be forced to live with it forever. By comparison, North Idaho College's and the College of Southern Idaho's levies fall between $80 and $100 per $100,000 of the assessed property value. As it turns out, the board now finds itself extremely challenged financially to build a new institution while serving the burgeoning demand from students.

Armed with the survey data, Micron Corporation directed Mike to do everything possible to get a community college up and running. Knowing about the impressive work the Albertson Foundation was doing, he presented them with the survey results. Both Micron and the JKAF had given up on the legislature, and in addition JKAF did not feel the proposals from BSU and TVCC were quite what they were looking for. At that meeting, they decided the only recourse was to go to the voters directly to try to set up a community college district. Also at that meeting members of the JKAF asked Mike if he knew anyone who could run a successful campaign; his response was that he knew just the right person.

At the same time that Micron and the JKAF were preparing to join forces, I mentioned earlier that the Nampa Chamber of Commerce decided to present a petition to the citizens of Ada and Canyon counties to see if they could get the required number of signatures to put the issue on the ballot. It didn't take long for M.C. Niland, of the Nampa Chamber, to join forces with Mike.

Petition to Form Community College District (pursuant to Idaho Code sec. 33-2104)

By signing this petition I am expressing my support for the formation of a community college district. The proposed district will consist of two counties, specifically Ada County and Canyon County. The district is to be known as the College of Western Idaho District. Those signing this petition state they are residents of one of the two counties in the proposed district and that they are qualified electors in a school district located in the proposed community college district. Those signing this petition ask that the counties of Ada and Canyon be organized into a community college district as described above.

	Printed Name	Address	City	School District	Signature	Date	Phone/Email (Optional)
1							
2							
3							
4							
5							
6							
7							
8							
9							
10							

I ________________, the affiant, am a qualified elector of the ________________ School District, located in ________________ County, and hereby verify that the above signed individuals are qualified electors whose names are signed to the petition or petitions have the qualification of school district electors and are residents of the proposed community college school district.

Signature: ____________________ Date: ________

STATE OF IDAHO)
) ss.
County of ________)

On this _____ day of _________, 2007, before me, the undersigned, a Notary Public in and for said State, personally appeared ________________, known or identified to me to be the person whose name is subscribed to the within instrument and acknowledges to me that he signed the same.

IN WITNESS WHEREOF, I have hereunto set my hand and affixed my official seal the day and year in this certificate first above written.

____
NOTARY PUBLIC FOR IDAHO
Residing at:
Commission expires:

Petition form

As I said before: Taking this bold action seemed to fly in the face of logic.

We were just entering a recession, and voters in Idaho are traditionally very "anti-tax" in their approach toward government. On top of that, if the referendum failed, all of the nay-sayers would simply crow that they knew all along there would be a negative backlash and many political leaders would have an excuse to continue to do nothing.

The petition required 1,000 signatures, but the people working on the campaign gathered more than 3,200 in record time. It was presented to the State Board of Education, as is required by state code, where it was approved overwhelmingly. The petition then went to Ada and Canyon county election officials and a referendum was scheduled for May 22, 2007.

Mike Reynoldson asked Jason Lehosit, who had experience managing campaigns, to run this one. In February 2007, Mike and Jason approached Mike Tracy of Tracy Communications who began to work on a marketing/media campaign strategy. In March, Jason hired a staff consisting of Shauneen Grange and Tara Wolfson, Field Directors; Keith Bybee, Stephen Goodson and Zach Hauge, Field Staff; Art Swift, Communications Director; and Penny Ysursa, Treasurer.

Mike and Jason then picked a group of community leaders who they thought could direct the effort, leaning on heavy hitters who could raise money. Their choice as Campaign Co-Chairs was Jerry Hess, Gary Michael, M.C. Niland and Skip Oppenheimer. Hatch Barrett, Guy Hurlbutt, Jerry Gunstream and Skip Smyser were named as finance co-chairs. These leaders represented both counties.

On March 1, 2007, the campaign officially kicked off with a lunch gathering of over 200 people in downtown Boise. Considerable enthusiasm and high expectations infused the crowd after a rousing speech from Governor Otter plus a number of other speakers.

The governor talked about how "sustaining our economic growth in Idaho means developing a qualified workforce—that means providing educational opportunities for everyone, not just those bound for universities." He discussed the fact that Idaho has a good high school graduation rate, but too few go on to college because sometimes they can't afford it and other times they're not interested in the kind of careers that require a four-year degree.

He explained further that, "today's kids need a chance, too. And now we have a Master Plan for a new community college right here in the Treasure Valley. It starts with a pledge of $5 million from Idaho taxpayers to get the ball rolling—but that's just the start. Now it's your turn. You'll find pledge forms here and folks ready and willing to collect them from you."

The governor was passionate about the need for a community college because he had started at Boise Junior College and after completing his first two years, matriculated to the College of Idaho where he graduated and became a Vice President for the J. R. Simplot Co., in charge of international markets. He, like so many others, came from a large family that didn't have a lot of money, and junior college opened the door to a whole new world for him and he never forgot it. He was a big advocate for community colleges in Idaho from the very beginning of his administration and continued to show that advocacy during the fund-raising campaign and throughout the whole effort to bring CWI into reality.

A plea for volunteers went out—the campaign needed people and funds—and the request for help drew a heartwarming response.

Ultimately, a little more than $380,000 was raised for the campaign during the next three months. More than 400 people contributed and the donations ranged from $5 to $50,000.

Mike Tracy, along with his partner Tom Donahoe, came up with all the concepts and production of campaign materials. They adopted the slogan "Give Me a Chance." "Community College Yes" became the campaign name. Tracy Communications also produced all the TV and radio spots, banners, and brochures.

The materials and advertising proved to be highly effective. People were inundated with messages in favor of the measure on the May ballot.

Campaign materials courtesy of Mike Tracy

Give me a
CHANCE
Many students must move away to get the classes they want and need at a rate they can afford.
COMMUNITY COLLEGE YES

Give me a
CHANCE
Among Idaho 9th graders, only
34% go on to college, and only
14% graduate within six years.
COMMUNITY
COLLEGE
YES

Give me a
CHANCE
In 2007, Idaho is graduating
only about half of the new nurses
we currently need statewide.
COMMUNITY
COLLEGE
YES

COMMUNITY
COLLEGE
YES
Give us a CHANCE
Vote May 22

Knowing it would be an uphill battle to pass the referendum, Jason and his staff developed a strategy of trying to convince all the voters likely to say yes to vote early by absentee ballot. A network of people gave brochures to individuals they thought would support the ballot measure and the last page of that brochure was a self-addressed post card they could fill out to have a ballot mailed to them.

I, like so many others, took these brochures out to professional organizations, civic clubs, and any other groups we could identify, as well as to individuals. In addition, more than 30,000 brochures were delivered to targeted homes, resulting in more than 12,000 returns. The cards were sent back to campaign headquarters, where they were recorded, bundled and given to election officials in both counties who mailed out the ballots. Jason and his people tracked those voters who didn't return their ballots and they were sent as many as four reminders. The ballot return rate proved to be extremely high.

By all accounts this strategy made the difference and it is generally agreed that the initiative would most likely have failed had the people running the campaign simply relied on getting the voters to the polls on the day of the referendum.

During the time between the kickoff on March 1 and the referendum on May 22, 2007, people were flooded with information about the advantages of a new comprehensive community college for the Treasure Valley.

Key leaders wrote opinion pieces to the papers. In a guest opinion in the *Idaho Statesman* on May 13, 2007, Dr. Stan Olson, Superintendent of the Boise School District and Dr. Linda Clark, Superintendent of the Meridian School District co-wrote an article which they concluded by appealing to voters "to join [them] in supporting the community college initiative. After all if we as a community do not provide this life-changing opportunity, who will?"

Both the *Statesman* and the *Idaho Press-Tribune* endorsed the referendum and there was an amazing coming together of people of both political parties and wide economic interests.

A persistent but minimal number of people opposed to the school wrote letters to the editor of both newspapers and protested through other sources. Their arguments centered on issues such as concern about the expansion of government, belief that business should pay for any workforce training the new school would offer, that taxes were already too high, and they didn't trust the cost figures being used in the campaign, and that Treasure Valley Community College from Ontario, Oregon, could take care of the workforce training needed for the burgeoning high tech industry in the Snake River Valley.

A quick note about Treasure Valley Community College (TVCC). TVCC is a first-rate, well-run institution in Ontario that developed a satellite operation in Caldwell several years ago. I applaud them for seeing a need and trying to fill it. The city of Caldwell embraced them and developed a great partnership. The problem with TVCC fulfilling the education and training needs of the entire valley is that by code, they couldn't spend any Oregon taxpayer dollars in Idaho nor could they expect to get any Idaho funds. Consequently, the classes had to be totally self-supporting—meaning that student fees had to cover the costs of facilities, teachers' salaries, administration, etc. That works for an academic survey course, i.e. English Composition, U.S. History, etc. It does not work well for many of the other courses that don't generate large numbers of students. The other problem is that to be able to offer professional-technical programs there is a considerable cost in equipment and labs for comparatively few students. Funding such programs solely through student fees is virtually impossible.

The city of Caldwell is currently building a facility downtown that they will lease back to TVCC and I believe that TVCC has proven they are doing good things given their constraints, and they will continue to be a good partner for CWI.

In advance of the Idaho community college district election, a considerable build-up of publicity and tension developed. On election night, people were guardedly optimistic, but remained anxious because of the required two-thirds majority vote. The Idaho electorate is conservative, and candidates often get elected to public office by simply stressing less government and no new taxes. That same electorate is normally, to say the least, suspicious of any new taxing district.

The numbers bounced around throughout the evening. The large gathering at election night headquarters at the Idaho Center waited and watched with more than a little trepidation. Toward the end of the evening, the vote hovered just short of the two-thirds majority until election officials opened the absentee ballots.

When we realized the referendum had passed we were, of course, ecstatic. Ada County approved it by 70.53% and Canyon County by 62.18%. Since more people voted in Ada County, the overall percentage of victory was 68.40%. All of the hard work had paid off. After the election results, I heard some grumbling from a few Canyon County folks about the measure not getting the two-thirds required vote in their county and having it "shoved down their throats once again by Ada County folks". I took great pleasure in reminding them that more than 62% of the people in Canyon County did, in fact, approve the measure and by any standard that's pretty impressive for a pro-tax vote.

After the votes were counted, there was a coming together of a large cross section of both Ada and Canyon county people who worked together to support the fledgling college. Several people who initially opposed the measure subsequently became supporters.

One of the most exciting things that happened was that the J.A. and Kathryn Albertson Foundation pledged $10 million to the College of Western Idaho nine days after the vote.

5 The Team

After the referendum passed, many people closely involved with the unexpected birth of a new community college felt a sense of high expectation. The first order of business was to seat a Board of Trustees. Under Idaho code when a new community college district is formed, the State Board of Education (SBOE) appoints the first Board of Trustees and they then stand for voter review at the next regular election.

SBOE invited people to apply to serve on the board. The response was enormous.

One hundred and one people applied—with 81 from Ada County and 20 from Canyon County. The state board faced the tough task of sorting through all the names and choosing five individuals who would be able to tackle this all important and monumental task of starting the college. The applicants comprised a cross-section of people from all facets of life.

Ultimately, SBOE selected five talented people. Chosen from Ada County was Guy Hurlbutt who, while retired, served as the President of the Idaho Business Coalition for Education Excellence and had been the former Chairman of the Idaho Education Alliance. He had enjoyed a successful career as a Vice President at Boise Cascade as well as the U.S. Attorney for the District of Idaho along with serving on the Selland Advisory Committee. Also chosen was Mark Dunham, who at that time was the Vice President of the Association of Commerce and Industry and former CEO of the Idaho Association of Realtors. He also had served as the Director of

Government Relations and Interim Vice President of Advancement at Boise State University. The third member of the group from Ada County was S. Hatch Barrett, President and CEO of Trebar, Inc. Among many other posts, Hatch served on the Boise State Foundation Board and the BSU Selland College Advisory Council. All three had a long history of community service and support for education.

From Canyon County Jerry Hess, a longtime successful entrepreneur and owner of J.M. Hess Construction, Inc., was selected. He had served in numerous leadership positions, including the Micron Technology Board of Directors, the Idaho State Board of Education, and as a board member of the Associated General Contractors.

The other Canyon County member was M.C. Niland, President and CEO of Western Idaho Training Company, and former Chairman of the Board of the Nampa Chamber of Commerce. She also has served on numerous community boards to include the Boise Airport Commission, the 3rd District Magistrates Commission, the Idaho State Council on Developmental Disabilities and the Idaho Division of Vocational Rehabilitation Advisory Council. Both of the Canyon County board members reflected a proven history of community service and support for education.

On July 30, 2007, the new board was sworn in by Milford Terrell, President of the State Board of Education. With the three from Ada County and two from Canyon County, there was a fair split representing the difference in population. But more importantly, all five people were intelligent, committed, and worked well together. It always amazed me that five individuals could be thrown together with such a herculean task ahead of them and proceed to work so well through many complicated and controversial issues. They didn't just work through them, but they did so while observing respect and dignity for each other. Probably the most exciting thing for me was that no one had a personal agenda; there was no grinding of axes. They were professional and objective.

Jerry Hess was elected chairman and proved to be a fine take-charge leader. He brought a definite entrepreneurial, can-do approach although driven by a certain amount of impatience regarding the system we all had to work within. He was a good listener and as a lifelong resident of Treasure Valley, his connections proved invaluable. He had a good knowledge of how the education system in Idaho worked as a result of having served on both the Nampa School Board and the State Board of Education. He insisted we start a college advisory committee that proved to be exactly what was needed. He also felt strongly about the need to gear up to help adult basic education students (those needing basic skills such as help with reading, writing, math, etc.) and really pushed for online learning. Even though he had little post-secondary education, he was well read in terms of, among other things, the future of education and training and its connection to the electronic age. He wanted to jump right into that whole arena and I was challenged helping him understand that while we planned to do just that, we first had to get the infrastructure in place. And that would take some time.

Mark Dunham was named vice chairman. He had experience working at BSU where he reported to Bob Kustra. He brought a thoughtful and analytical presence to the board and his real estate experience proved useful in all our facilities transactions. He had been a longtime lobbyist and was well known by Idaho politicians. Mark was detail oriented and his writing and editing skills proved to be useful. He brought a needed balance by helping the other board members understand what we could and couldn't do within the educational/political system and helped as a liaison with BSU particularly when they questioned some decisions we made.

M.C. Niland was asked to serve as secretary/treasurer. She had been instrumental in the campaign to get the referendum passed and believed strongly in what we were doing. She immersed herself in the financials and worked closely with Cheryl Wright to mold them into a format the board could work with. She required data on all subjects to back up any discussions and studied the findings carefully. She was a passionate advocate for the college offering programs and opportunities for the developmentally disabled segment of our community and for community education (personal enrichment) classes in general and had difficulty understanding why they couldn't happen right away. Again, I had to assure her that such programs would happen, but not until the infrastructure was in place.

Guy Hurlbutt was the fourth member of the board. He too, was instrumental in helping pass the referendum. He brought a calm, rational approach to issues and his background as an attorney came in extremely handy as we worked through many complicated transactions. He was a good and thoughtful listener. His contacts in the community were vast and proved quite helpful. He handled the many disagreements and inevitable intense board discussions in a dignified manner. He and Mark were especially concerned about the number of BSU people I brought in to jump start the college. I had to spend time helping them understand why I used that approach and that the new people did fully understand the community college mission—we wouldn't become a "miniature version of BSU." After the election, in November 2008, he was chosen as the next chairman of the board and did a superb job.

The fifth member of the original board was Hatch Barrett. Hatch brought a dignified, calm presence. He didn't say a lot, but when he did, it was always spot on and he definitely added to the discussion. He brought the most knowledge of professional-technical education to the board because he was a longtime supporter and benefactor of the Selland College of Applied Technology at BSU. His business experience and ties to the community were also useful and appreciated. He was the one board member who would often refer to me when they would get into an involved discussion about college operations or policies with a statement such as, "let's ask Dennis, he's the expert—that's why we hired him." I always appreciated that, because in their enthusiasm the board would, at times, appear to forget that with my executive staff and me all in the room at every board meeting, they had a modicum of resources available.

Founding board members.

Left to right: Jerry Hess, M.C. Niland, Guy Hurlbutt, Mark Dunham, Hatch Barrett

(Courtesy of CWI)

The hurdles that this group of dedicated and highly competent professionals had to jump when they first gathered seemed overwhelming as they settled in and contemplated the immense task ahead. They were charged with starting a community college from scratch and had a lot riding on the endeavor. All their considerable reputations were at stake. They were closely watched and felt the pressure and some criticism from the community. As I mentioned earlier, we had nothing to start with—no address, no phone number, no employees, no facilities, and no money. They sought advice from a number of sources and decided that hiring a new president should be the first order of business.

The trustees knew there would be a number of complicated legal issues to work through. They went to the law firm of Eberle Berlin Kading Turnbow & McKlveen, Chartered for that assistance, and Rich Stover was assigned as our attorney. Rich proved to be committed and competent and was invaluable to both the board and to me. He attended every board meeting during that first two years and helped us work through literally dozens of memorandums of agreement and contracts.

This is where I entered the picture.

I was hired as president on August 7, 2007. I, too, knew that I had to quickly surround myself with a competent executive staff.

I faced the challenge of offering classes at Idaho's newest college as soon as possible, but enjoyed the luxury of having highly qualified professionals available to me from BSU's Selland College of Applied Technology. Nevertheless I felt pressure from some of our board members and various influential individuals and organizations to ensure that CWI simply not be a "miniature version of BSU." There were doubts by some in the community that since I had been at BSU for 18 years that I really understood the role and mission of a community college either operationally or philosophically, so starting out with six BSU staff members didn't allay their fears. Several members of the board really struggled with these and subsequent hires from BSU, along with other issues that boiled over during the next two years.

The board had a huge challenge, to say the least. They had to get to know each other and to learn to communicate with each other while overseeing this daunting undertaking. A board which administers a mature college essentially has five primary responsibilities: 1) Hire and hold responsible a President, 2) approve and monitor a budget, 3) approve major purchases and acquisitions, 4) set policy and make sure it is carried out and 5) approve all higher level hires. In our case, however, the board, correctly I believe, took a much more hands-on approach. I believe that was motivated, in part, by their need to be comfortable that my staff and I knew what we were doing. While I understood that, I have to say it became frustrating trying to do the things we needed to do in a timely manner and having even basic operational decisions second-guessed and debated sometimes in a seemingly endless manner. We realized that they were seeing things from a strategic point of view (i.e. creating a 21st Century College) and what a mature institution ought to look like. The trustees exhibited impatience, at times, that my team and I appeared to them to be floundering. I had to keep reminding them that we were struggling to build an enormous infrastructure just to get the college operational.

We all went through a period of testing each other and having to learn to trust.

I remember early in the whole process, the board and my staff were struggling with the strategic plan over several sessions lasting long hours. We had a facilitator running the meetings and she worked diligently to create a non-threatening atmosphere so people would feel free to say whatever was on their minds. In the first couple of sessions, the board lined up on one side of the table and my team on the other, contributing to the perception of separation that my managers felt already existed. My executive team came away from the early sessions frustrated because they didn't feel safe to speak their minds.

As a group, we hadn't yet evolved to the point where we could trust enough to be open with each other. As their trust in my team and me grew and our trust in them increased, that dynamic evolved. The tension gradually lessened so that by the time Guy became the chairman the second year, the board meetings shortened and the whole process became more relaxed, efficient, and streamlined.

Even though at times there was tension causing anxiety between me and various individuals on the board and with the board in general, I have to say that given the enormous pressures we all felt and the huge task we all shared, we always worked things out. I look back on my experiences with the board with fond memories and came to realize that definite stages of group dynamics had to take place for this institution to become a reality. What we all went through was entirely normal and I think we all had great respect for each other when I left for retirement.

The first person to join me was my longtime management assistant, Debbie Jensen, who had been at BSU for 14 years, the last eight working with me. She had proven to be a loyal and competent professional. She assisted me as I managed the West Campus and the Canyon County Center for BSU. In fact she was instrumental in opening the new West Campus Classroom facility for BSU in 2005. It was a leap of faith for her to leave BSU and become part of this adventure, but she proved to be a valuable member of my team.

I knew that the financial side of our new operation would be critical and needed to be addressed immediately. The first manager I brought on was Cheryl Wright who became our Vice President for Finance and Administration. Cheryl had more than 30 years of accounting and management experience. She had served in several budgeting and finance capacities for eight years at BSU with the last three as Business Manager for the Larry Selland College of Applied Technology, where she oversaw a budget of $12.8 million. She understood the state budgeting system and public accounting, and more importantly, she wasn't afraid to ask others throughout the state for advice and didn't feel intimidated in the process. She was eager to join us and did a great job. She brought to the group strong attention to detail and a good memory that kept us on track.

The next person I hired was Dr. Victor Watson as Executive Vice President in charge of Instruction and Student Services. Victor had worked for both four-year and community colleges in two other states before coming to Idaho. In fact, he had been through two other start-ups before taking on this endeavor. He had served as both an associate provost for instruction and student services as well as a dean of a college along with service as a registrar. He came to Idaho to retire but decided he wasn't through working and was then hired as Associate Dean, Enrollment Management and Student Services at the Larry Selland College of Applied Technology. I was elated when he decided to join our team, because he had the most experience of any of my team members working directly for a community college and he proved to be worth his weight in gold. His calm demeanor was important to the dynamic of our group, while his sense of humor was delightful; often he would revert to his pure Texas dialect with some off-the-wall witticism that put us all in stitches at just the right time to relieve tension. Other than me, he was also the one person that anyone on my team could talk to and get good advice and counsel.

Brian Currin was hired as our Executive Director of Information Technology and Facilities. Brian had experience in the private sector as well as with BSU. I thought it crucial that information technology (IT) be part of our planning from the very beginning. IT has become pervasive in every aspect of higher education and it had to be central to all of our strategic planning. At BSU, Brian was the Director of Information Technology for the Larry Selland College of Applied Technology for 12 years. He handled the IT infrastructure and related classroom issues for the college. He also worked closely with the Dean of the Selland College on infrastructure surrounding facilities and classrooms. Brian was an important and valued member of our team. He, too, had a great sense of humor; he would sit back and observe a debate for a while and then throw in a zinger just at the appropriate moment.

The next person I brought aboard was Cathy Hampton. Cathy had 37 years experience at BSU, the last 18 of those as the Special Assistant to the Dean of the Selland College with expertise in project management, human resource management, and budget preparation and oversight. Cathy was an integral part of our team because she had the institutional memory and knowledge of the Selland College and helped us enormously as we worked through the complicated process of transitioning all the Selland employees out of BSU and the state system and merging them into ours. She also compiled many special reports and conducted needed research. She wasn't afraid to say what needed to be said, even though at times we may not have wanted to hear it. Her insights were always right on target and much appreciated, later at least if not at the moment she said it.

The last person to join my executive team was Shirl Boyce. Shirl was our Executive Director of Community Relations and Advancement. Previously, he had worked at the Boise Metro Chamber of Commerce to build the Boise Area Economic Development Council into a respected professional economic development movement for the Boise area (later renamed the Boise Valley Economic Partnership). He was the Executive Director and was later named Vice President for Economic Development where he served for more than 20 years. For 10 years, Shirl was on the Selland College of Applied Technology's Advisory Council, serving for a time as its chair.

He held numerous positions in state government, including working directly for two governors. He was well known not only in the Treasure Valley, but throughout the state and was widely respected. When he was asked to join the CWI team he was serving as Development Director for the Selland College. Shirl's community perspective was vital—he seemed to know what would fly or not with the public, and he brought a high level of energy to the team.

Already discussed, was the fact that I received some criticism for raiding the BSU staff, partly generated by concerns that we would be creating a mini-BSU, but I stuck to my guns. I had what I considered two excellent reasons for choosing this path. The first was the time constraint. Had I opted for a national search for these positions, it would have taken months, perhaps as long as a year and we were already feeling the heat to make things happen as soon as possible. After decades of waiting for this college to materialize, we were all ready to see it up and running as soon as possible.

The other reason I selected these men and women was because they were all eminently qualified. I can't imagine that I would have found a better staff if I had done a national search. These people could all hit the ground running, and they did.

"Founding Executive Team"

Left to right: Cathy Hampton, Cheryl Wright, Brian Currin, Dennis Griffin, Shirl Boyce, Victor Watson, Debbie Jensen

(Courtesy of CWI)

As to fears that we really didn't understand the difference between a university and a community college and we would end up simply being a smaller version of BSU, let me offer the following.

Even though the Selland College operated as a college within the university and the dean of that college reported to the provost at BSU, the Selland College functioned semi-autonomously in that they had their own funds and budget sent directly to them by the State Division of Professional-Technical Education. They had to account for the funds and report regularly to the state separately from BSU. The college had always provided the professional-technical aspect of BSU's community college mission for the southwest region of Idaho.

In addition, the dean of the Selland College, even though she reported to the BSU Provost, also reported to the Director of the State Division for Professional-Technical Education. The last aspect was that they were the only college at BSU with an open admissions policy (one of the tenants of a community college). The staff and faculty had worked with community college type students for 60 years and they were eager to bring their knowledge and skills to a full-fledged community college.

The point is that these fine professionals that I imported from the Selland College to serve as my executive team and the people they brought from Selland College, clearly understood what a community college was and went about the work of getting CWI's doors open in record time.

6 The Clock Ticks

The crew in place, I had two years to get the college humming with the sound of students before my contract ended in August 2009, and I planned to retire.

Two years may seem like a long time, but that's a matter of perspective. We were already fielding questions about "why didn't we have classes up and running a month after the referendum passed." I responded by saying unless you're in the middle of such a project you simply have no clue as to the complexities we faced. Even though we were all professionals who had been involved in higher education for many years and were far from clueless, we too had much more to learn, particularly in the arena of politics and state processes.

What transpired between August 2007 and August 2009 turned out to be the thrill ride of a lifetime. Being named president of a college was an honor for about 10 minutes—until I realized that I had been appointed to take the rudder of a non-existent ship and I had to draw the blueprint as well as build the ship.

Before I hired an executive team I had to negotiate my own contract with the Board of Trustees. That process went smoothly and I felt the board was fair. Guy Hurlbutt tells the story about visiting relatives in Seattle and riding along the freeway with a car full of family members while he was on the cell phone negotiating with me and our attorney to finalize my contract. I think this sort of "operating on the fly" was typical of what we all did much of that two-year span.

Then I had to resign as executive director of BSU West and negotiate with BSU to stay on the state benefits package until we could get our own benefits plan established. The board thankfully accommodated that request.

We quite literally were starting from scratch, and many of the things we take for granted with any job did not exist for this new community college—basics such as offices for the staff, telephones, office equipment, and the funding mechanism to pay for these things had to be obtained and set up. We also had to set up the basic business and administrative mechanisms, such as our state and federal business filings and tax identification.

Once more, BSU was willing to work with us and allowed me to remain in the BSU West facility in addition to providing offices there for my team. Dr. Sona Andrews, BSU's Provost and Vice President of Academic Affairs, proved to be supportive and helpful during this process. In the meantime, my assistant, Debi Jensen, kept herself more than busy getting phones, computers, copiers, and all the office supplies lined up. She also had to set up the billing process so that we could use BSU's equipment until we could find a way to pay for our own. Since we now had an address, at least for the time being, we ordered stationary and business cards. The board had already applied for and we soon received a federal tax identification number from the IRS.

We were now "official", at least in some ways, but we soon learned that the real challenges were still gathering steam.

I had already negotiated with BSU to declare the executive team members as "loaned employees" for a time, which also allowed them to remain on the state benefits package. To do that, they had to sign an agreement that if something unforeseen happened they could not return to BSU. I started August 7, 2007, and by the end of the month everyone on the team had climbed aboard what began to feel like a leaky raft tossed on a stormy sea.

We were a hearty crew though, and our first weeks were spent in day-long meetings brain-storming all the issues we needed to address. We prioritized tasks and assigned them to the people I believed could form the various spokes of the all-important academic wheel. While we were excited about the opportunity we had been given, the multitude of tasks that lay ahead seemed overwhelming.

I would be remiss if I didn't admit that I was getting a steady stream of unsolicited advice from a variety of people (none of whom, of course, had ever started a college). The good thing about all of the input was that it showed me that members of the valley communities were charged up and eager for the college to start admitting students. I learned to listen politely and sift through the suggestions while relying on our collective experience, and to simply trust my team and my "gut" in most cases.

On top of all the advice and rather intense scrutiny, the job was a 24/7 kind of endeavor. If I wasn't working on all that had to be done, I was thinking about it. It was almost impossible to get my mind off the project.

I remember going on a week-long trip to Hawaii a few months after we all started to get into the swing of things. I felt guilty even going, but the tickets and rooms had been booked before I took the job and Chairman Hess encouraged me to go. Here I was in "paradise" and much of the time, my mind was on CWI. I found myself sitting on the veranda of our room with an ocean breeze and palm trees swaying, making regular calls to see how things were going. In retrospect, that was crazy, but my whole team felt that way—we were committed to making this project work and producing something special. Looking back I don't know what I would have done without my wife, Joni, who kept me grounded and to keep things in perspective. Her advice and counsel were invaluable.

I focused first on the financial side of our endeavor. Governor Otter and the legislature had approved $5 million as seed money for our startup and soon advanced the initial $600,000. We had to develop a business plan to get the remaining $4.4 million. As a result of the bad timing in getting started, we were already behind in the state budget cycle.

Dr. Jerry Beck, President of the College of Southern Idaho, called right after my appointment and offered his help for anything we needed. Knowing that Mike Mason, his Chief Financial Officer, was regarded as one of the experts in the state on community college finance, I asked if he could come right away and spend some time with Cheryl Wright, our Vice President for Finance and Administration, and me to give us a tutorial and help us catch up. He agreed and not only spent all the time we requested but also brought a thick binder of instructions and samples of the information we needed. The offers of help such as that provided by Jerry Beck and his team are what helped us create the solid foundation for our new adventure.

Cheryl went to work formulating our first budget. She not only had to prepare the budget for the current year (2007-08), but the budget for fiscal year 2008-09 was already late and both had to be submitted. There were dozens of details that had to go into those documents and we were really flying at warp speed. Having no history to work from made the entire process even more complicated. My team and I tried to visualize all the things we would need to bring CWI into reality such as facilities, capital purchases, office expenses, personnel, consultants, marketing (because we planned to start our first students in fall, 2008)—all the many facets of life required to birth a fledgling college. We had to gauge costs and timing of each such expense as the budget year unfolded—we epitomized "zero-based budgeting."

We had many more unknowns than knowns which made it difficult to build a reliable budget. Facilities were a problem. Would BSU continue to provide office space and if so, for how long? When would we need classrooms, how many, and where? Who would we need to hire, how many, and when? Would we be able to transfer the Selland College over by August 2008 as the board wanted, and if so what about facilities, and human resources? The list went on and on.

We spent several sessions reviewing the budget, and each time after Cheryl went back and crunched the numbers, we would start the exercise over. This process continued until at last we had pieced together a budget that seemed to work—based on a lot of assumptions.

After we glued the various budget figures into a whole package, we hired a consultant, Dr. Jerry Gee, former Vice President of Academic Affairs at North Idaho College, to help us write a business plan and he worked closely with Cheryl to bring it together. The team again went through repeated tweaking of the business plan until we were all satisfied.

Within weeks, we had both the budget and business plan on paper and presented them to the board of trustees for approval. I then appeared before the next regular meeting of the Idaho State Board of Education to present the figures and request the remainder of the $5 million that had been promised. Our planning was well received and funds were approved, so we put the seed money into a checking account.

We were actually in business!

Cheryl set up our initial accounting system in a "QuickBooks" software package and administered the accounts herself. Using QuickBooks was symbolic and very illustrative of how small we started and how far we came in just two years. That particular software package works well with small businesses and served us well for a short time. We came so far so fast that two years hence, we had grown into a $28 million dollar budget run by a sophisticated accounting system and a sizable department.

Without the initial funding, we simply could not have started because it would take another 16 months before we would receive any student tuition funds or property tax revenue. The $5 million seed money from the legislature, as a result of Governor Otter's request, was a God-send and we could not have turned the key to open the college doors without it. BSU agreed to do our payroll through August 2008 and our payables through June 2008. Again, this crucial partnership was greatly appreciated. The pledged financial support from JKAF would come at a later date.

One of the next things I focused on was accreditation—crucial to any educational institution. It led to some of the most sensitive moments in putting the college together.

A quick note about how critically important accreditation is to any institution.

It truly is the lifeblood of a college or university because in order for students to receive federal financial aid or for their credits to be transferable to another institution, accreditation must be in place. Once a new college gets an established partner, an application for consideration is written with input from both sides of the partnership.

For colleges and universities in the Northwest accreditation is granted by a regional association called the Northwest Commission on Colleges and Universities (NWCCU), headquartered in Seattle. In this region, new schools are allowed to partner with an existing accredited institution and "use" their accreditation status until the new school can stand on its own academic feet. We had planned to partner with Boise State University.

When NWCCU approves the application, a self-study is initiated and takes one to two years. After that is submitted and approved an initial candidacy visit is scheduled (usually three years from the time the process starts). If the inspection by members of the NWCCU is successful (In other words, are you doing what you said you were doing on the self study.) an expanded visit is scheduled by the accreditation agency.

If all goes well, the institution is granted candidacy and allowed to issue its own federal financial aid without the process of having to team with the sponsoring college. There are two follow-up visits scheduled at 18 and 36 months. If everything continues to go well, a final visit is scheduled two years later and, providing all is well, the college would be granted its full accreditation. The final decision is made by the NWCCU Board of Commissioners.

You will notice that I use the word "if" a lot. It's unusual for this whole process to work flawlessly; there are inevitably complications which delay the college becoming independently accredited. Under the best conditions, the whole process takes six to seven years. When I left CWI in August 2009, we had just completed the application for consideration and were ready to submit it.

One of the first things I did to get work on accreditation moving was to schedule a meeting with NWCCU in Seattle. Dr. James Munger, the representative from BSU, Dr. Victor Watson (our Executive Vice President for Instruction and Student Affairs), Guy Hurlbutt, and I attended the meeting where we gained a lot of insight into the multi-year process on which we were embarking. And even though BSU was a willing partner, problems materialized that neither its leaders nor ours could have foreseen.

Boise State informed us early on that they simply would not be ready for a fall 2008 start (some 10 months hence) from an information technology and systems standpoint. At the same time, we were busily negotiating with them as to how to transfer the Selland College of Applied Technology to CWI. They proposed a transition stretching over three years along with an accreditation partnership. There were significant negative financial implications for us because BSU wanted $7.2 million dollars for the arrangement.

In the meantime, I arranged a meeting with Jerry Beck of the College of Southern Idaho and his vice president for instruction. I approached him regarding his earlier offer to help and asked if that offer included an accreditation partnership. Victor Watson also joined us for the meeting.

I had mixed feelings putting that meeting together. I heard many strong opinions from people urging me both ways (to stay with BSU or to partner with CSI), and I felt a little disloyal to BSU even talking with Jerry. I had a long history of working with the university and they had put a lot of work into various partnership proposals along with their strong expectation that we would partner with them.

Jerry assured me that he was quite willing to work with us in any way the College of Southern Idaho could. He offered specifically to be our partner in the accreditation endeavor and to do so at little cost and right away.

I had a major decision to make, and again I needed my team's input. We spent much of Saturday, New Years Eve 2007, at J.B.'s Restaurant in Meridian debating whether to ride the horse we started on or switch mounts. The team wrestled through several hours of discussion postulating solid arguments both ways but in the end they were nearly unanimous in their support of my ultimate proposal.

I decided to recommend to the board changing our accreditation partnership from BSU to CSI and also change our strategy of obtaining the Selland College from a "transition" approach to a total "transfer" approach with a date certain.

Such an about face did not come easily. I was a Boise State graduate, had worked for them for 18 years and bled blue and orange as a Bronco football fan. I had worked to build BSU's presence in western Treasure Valley both in terms of programs and facilities. I was, and still am, loyal to them, but did what I thought best for CWI's immediate and long term future.

The board approved my recommendation after long discussion. It was obvious there was a lot riding on this decision relative to community relations here in Treasure Valley and in our future partnership with Boise State. Victor and I met with Sona Andrews on a Saturday morning and I told her of our decision. She was shocked but after an awkward silence began to process the surprising news and did postulate that at least many at her institution would be relieved. We knew that was the case because the people running the various departments at BSU who would actually have to implement the partnership had told us that they were concerned they couldn't make it happen given the constraints we had laid on them. They were going through a significant information technology upgrade and to take us on would have been a major challenge during that overhaul.

For us, partnering with CSI was a much better fit in that they were a fellow community college, much smaller than BSU, and could deal with us without interrupting their operation significantly and at considerably less cost to us.

This unexpected shift did, however, send shock waves throughout the valley. Again I felt pressure from people who expressed strong beliefs both ways. Some felt we were abandoning BSU "after all they had done for us" (which was significant) and that we shouldn't partner with a school outside the valley. For others, the change made perfect sense because working with another community college was "what we should have been doing all along." As usual I got lots of advice (wanted and unwanted) but we had clearly set a course, which by the way, we never regretted. Victor fielded the accreditation ball, and ran with it, shepherding the process, which proved to be arduous and time consuming. Later in the process, he hired Dr. Stan Brings, who functioned ably as our Institutional Effectiveness Director, heading the accreditation effort.

As we planned our early moves, Victor and I looked at several organizational charts from colleges nationwide. We knew that to do valid planning, we first had to adopt an organizational model, and then each executive team member must forecast timing of the hiring. We needed to have people in place, trained, and ready to tackle their duties. The timing also involved putting the right people into the right jobs early enough to learn, load, and be able to use the new and unknown Enterprise Resource Planning (computer) System—a daunting undertaking.

Two tasks needing to be completed on our tight deadline seemed at first glance to be entirely frivolous: designing a logo and choosing school colors. Yet we all know the importance to staff, students, and alumni of these seemingly minor institutional identifiers.

Brian Currin, Executive Director of Facilities and Information Technology, was assigned the task of researching and recommending a logo and colors. He worked with a designer and they presented several choices for both. Brian made sure that no other educational institutions in the state sported the colors we proposed. The team reviewed several alternatives submitted by Brian and we finally settled on three logo designs (all of which depicted a compass with an arrow above pointing west). The colors we decided to recommend were brick red and light gold—the colors used in all of the "Community College Yes" campaign literature. Again, these were presented to our board and they approved our color suggestion and one of the logo proposals. We now could order letterhead stationery and begin to develop a marketing plan.

(Courtesy of CWI)

Shirl Boyce, Executive Director of Community Relations and Advancement, spearheaded the marketing plan.

He contracted with Red Sky Communications to draft the plan. Stephanie Worrell, CEO of Red Sky, and her staff, including Chad Biggs, proved to be effective and up to the task. Shirl spent many hours with the Red Sky team and this effort produced an innovative plan complete with marketing branding for our burgeoning college. Shirl developed a series of ongoing news releases and maintained regular communication with the media. He also developed an e-newsletter sent regularly to thousands of people of influence in the community. He spent a great deal of time developing and refining the web site, which required regular and ongoing meetings with various departmental staff in order to correctly reflect our services and provide accurate information to the public. He also laid the advancement groundwork, meeting with local people and groups with affluence and influence in the community who could help in the future.

Another important task for Shirl was to establish the College Advisory Council. The first committee included Tom Dale, Mayor of Nampa; June Gempler, Micron Technology; Burke Hansen, Hansen Rice, Inc.; Sam Haws; Chuck Hedemark; Jim Hogge, Idaho Small Business Development Center; Dwight Johnson, Idaho Department of Labor; Kevin Learned; Steve Millard, Idaho Hospital Association; and Ann Stephens, Director of the Idaho Division of Professional Technical Education. The committee was chaired by Paul Hiller—Executive Director of the Boise Valley Economic Development Council.

Shirl also designed outside signage for the main campus building, re-designed the signage entering the campus, and recommended names for the streets on the Nampa campus.

Cheryl took on the daunting task of building the "business infrastructure" of the college from scratch which involved, among other things, the development of a general ledger with a full chart of accounts, consisting of hundreds of headings, developing procedures for cash handling and financial reporting, developing departmental budgets and reporting taxes. She also had to develop internal controls, an accounts payable department, purchasing policies and procedures, purchase card policies and implementation, travel reimbursement procedures, fixed asset management, inventory control, student accounts policies and procedures, and bookstore operation among many other responsibilities.

Another major task Cheryl was asked to take on was Human Resources. She was placed in charge of the recruiting and selection process, developing position numbers, researching employee compensation and benefit packages, developing performance management procedures, an employee orientation program, equal employment opportunity data, and establishing a Safety Committee, to name only a few of the responsibilities that fall under HR.

Additionally Cheryl was named our election official. Even though the original five trustees were chosen by SBOE, code stipulated that they must stand for election at the next regular voting date.

After that the slate of leaders was to be placed on staggered terms. The board members run at-large meaning that by code they do not represent any specific area within the two-county taxing district. There has been talk since in the legislature about changing that.

Two of the original board members, Jerry Hess and Hatch Barrett, chose not to stand for election, but the three remaining members did. Cheryl had to work with our attorney to coordinate all the details with election officials from both counties.

The election was held in November 2008, and the three incumbents, Guy Hurlbutt, Mark Dunham, and M.C. Niland were all elected.

The two new board members voted in to replace Jerry Hess and Hatch Barrett were Stan Bastian and Tammy Ray, both of whom turned out to be excellent choices and dedicated to making the college the very best it could be.

Stan Bastian

Tammy Ray

(Courtesy of CWI)

Victor was responsible for setting up the student services department. This included: procedures for enrolling and registering students, a catalog, financial aid procedures, marketing materials, guidelines for student governance, student disability services, and student grievance procedures. Since we were "using" the College of Southern Idaho's accreditation, he had to coordinate a laundry list of start-up procedures including making sure that our curriculum aligned with theirs—a juggling act, especially regarding the Selland College programs. We were also required by CSI to also register our students on their system, so Victor was in charge of coordinating dual computer systems—a project that of course did not smoothly fall into place.

Another vast (and critical) function that fell under Victor's purview was instruction. He was responsible for developing a class schedule, recommending criteria for beginning salaries for the faculty, setting up placement testing, establishing library services, and creating a process to develop a vision and goals for general education, professional-technical education, developmental education, workforce training, community education, concurrent enrollment, and other educational programs.

I have to say, again, that the College of Southern Idaho was quite helpful, cooperative and supportive. They took a real risk in partnering with us. They put their accreditation on the line, and without such unqualified support, we could not have offered credit transferable courses or federal financial aid for years.

Within a few months of coming on board, Victor, Cheryl, and Brian began hiring some key people needed to get right to work establishing the systems to build the college. Victor soon hired a Dean of Enrollment and Student Services, Terry Blom; a Registrar, Connie Black; a Director of Financial Aid, Kevin

Jensen; and within a few months an Associate Vice President for Instruction, Dr. Rick Aman.

Cheryl hired a Controller, Marilyn Griggs; Human Resources and Payroll Manager, Janet Baxter; and an assistant, Jennifer Hedges. Brian Currin brought on board Developer Analyst Lead, Kim Channpraseut; two Systems Engineers, Chris Smith and Tom Peppersack; and an E-Learning and Multimedia Services Lead, Mark Westcott. Many others came on board quickly and all proved to be dedicated qualified professionals. Some of the additional leaders were Dr. Marilyn Martin, Director of Workforce Development; Barbara Case, Director of Community Education; and Jac Webb, Director of Adult Basic Education, who later came to us with the transfer of the Selland College.

As I mentioned, many of the early employees came from the Selland College. While the board did accept the early hires, with some reservation, they made it clear that we were to expand our searches beyond the boundaries of BSU and the Selland College. They felt pressure from some individuals and organizations in the community and felt as well that we wouldn't be able to develop our own culture with all the BSU influence. We did then develop nation-wide searches, but in many cases, the stronger candidates were right here.

One incident I will never forget.

We presented a slate of new-hire candidates to the board for their review prior to one board meeting. We listed where they came from and while we did have some out-of-town candidates, most again were from BSU. I received a phone call from Guy Hurlbutt on a Sunday afternoon prior to our regular monthly meeting scheduled for the following Tuesday. He said he was just letting me know that at the meeting he intended to take me to task.

When we came to the agenda item dealing with the new hires, he looked right at me and said, "Dennis, I don't know whether you didn't hear me or whether you chose to ignore me, but this list of primarily BSU people is not acceptable." He felt so strongly about the issue that there was no doubt he was angry with me. He said it in a way that only a good lawyer can and I really felt on the defensive. I was taken aback, because I have great respect for Guy and never before or since have I seen him so upset. A long discussion ensued and I again tried to point out our predicament. Do we hire out-of-town people simply because they're from out of town, or do we hire the best people we can?

Guy handled the discussion with grace. We were both able to state our positions and respectful discussion followed. We didn't talk about it right afterwards but have more recently where we both got a chuckle from the memory. Like so many other intense discussions, we all got past this and my team redoubled their efforts to find good candidates from other than BSU and hired many.

In fact our Associate Vice President for Instruction, and Director of Financial Aid both came from Oregon community colleges. Our Director of Human Resources came from the City of Boise. Most of the employees in the student services area and the finance area came from several other colleges and private business. Our entire full-time academic/credit transfer faculty did not come from BSU nor did most of our adjunct faculty members.

I have never regretted my decision, to start with the cadre of BSU/Selland College key people. Early on, we were able to get off to a much faster start bringing the college on line than if we had to go through national searches for those positions.

There were certainly other areas of debate and even contention at times. The board really wanted us to start for-credit academic classes in August 2008, and we agreed to try to do that. As it turned out, we simply weren't ready and informed the board. They strongly voiced their concern and a couple of them said that they had already told people we would be starting on that date. After a lot of questions and comments, they accepted the reality of the situation and we moved past it.

Another issue was that of writing a policy manual. We went to a lot of expense and spent a great deal of time putting one together for their approval. Cathy Hampton took the lead on this, and did an excellent job of keeping all the versions up to date and coordinated, and we hired Jerry Gee to help us with the original drafts. He reviewed the manuals at both the College of Southern Idaho and North Idaho College and melded them into the key policies and procedures he felt we needed to get started. My team then went through everything and further refined the manual.

The board took his and our work and discussed, at length, the way in which it should have been done (some wanted it to be reflective of a corporate manual) and others wanted to follow more in line with what an academic institution does. We had to go back through it several times and the board spent part of almost every meeting discussing issues within it. The whole discussion was arduous and was still ongoing at the time of my retirement.

The faculty handbook provided yet another contentious and ongoing discussion. We proposed one based on what the other two Idaho community colleges were doing and what is typically done. The board was convinced that there were several areas that needed work, especially favoring the stipulation that all faculty members should be hired on an "at will" basis. That created a huge problem for the new faculty we had already hired and for the Selland College faculty yet to be transferred to us. That issue is still unresolved.

There were other areas that generated long debate both among the board members and between them and me. But we treated each other with respect and the discussions were always handled in a professional manner. I admire how the board tackled many obstacles.

Very early in the process of laying the foundation for the community college, we had to decide on an Enterprise Resource Planning System (ERP)—in other words a computer system. Brian headed this complicated process. He did the research and found that two companies stood out in providing ERP services to community colleges, Jenzabar and Datatel. Brian had the two companies provide day-long presentations to the small staff we had at that point and to the Selland College of Applied Technology which was still part of BSU but would be transferring to us. In addition, a delegation from BSU including representatives from the Controller's Office, Student Services, and Office of Information Technology joined us. The computer representatives each did presentations to the Executive Team as well.

As we looked at other small four-year and community colleges throughout Idaho, in our opinion Datatel was the better system even though both systems were being used around the state. The team analyzed the data and one of the major decision points was that Datatel exhibited the best track record for larger schools, which we knew CWI would become in a few short years. Brian made a presentation to the Board listing the advantages and disadvantages of each, and they agreed with our assessment and approved our recommendation. By this time the first $5 million had been transferred to us from the state board, so we purchased it.

An ERP system is particularly crucial for an educational institution. It must have the capacity to potentially track tens of thousands of students—enrolling, registering, class rosters, grades, transcripts, financial aid, and numerous other things. Such a system must be capable of handling the business side of the house—accounting, budgeting, receivables, payables, payroll, etc. It must be a communication vehicle for all of the students, staff, and faculty, and it has to provide support for instructors in the classroom because virtually all of the courses we started out with had an "on-line" component if not offered entirely on-line. Datatel proved to work well providing these and many other state-of-the-art features.

When we bought the software, we also purchased the "fast start" option, which meant that we had a constant presence of consultants from Datatel training employees. Our entire growing group of employees was severely challenged spending hours in training and still doing all the other things needed to get the college operational. In the interest of time, we also asked Datatel to give us a "best practices" approach to get the system set up. They had seen many other operations and could help us establish one without making the same mistakes others had made and save us time.

Brian and his staff had their hands additionally full purchasing a server and finding a location in which to house it. They had to provide connectivity to what would ultimately become eight separate locations, even contracting to bore a conduit under the highway separating the main campus from the administrative offices. In addition, he had to develop a system for data storage, coordinate desktop technology, and select a system for electronic library collections, along with wireless technology in all locations plus a telecommunications system. An email address also was necessary. More details popped up that we had to work out and it all had to be coordinated and in place in time for the loading of our new ERP System and to train personnel on it.

At the same time, we embarked on a strategic planning process. We hired Hagler and Associates to direct the project. The principle, Kathy Hagler, and her partner Sally Anderson, proved to be exactly the right pair for the job. We asked that they take an abbreviated approach, once again in the interest of time constraints, and they performed admirably. They had done the strategic plan for the City of Boise and Boise State University. In each of those blueprints they were able to glean a modicum of data as to the need for a community college. We also put together a planning team made up of key members of the community to provide guidance and input. We held community input meetings called "Community Conversations." They consisted of day and evening sessions at the Civic Center in Nampa and at the Centre on the Grove in Boise. During the day we had invited guests representing a broad cross-section of the community, while the evening was opened up to the general public.

Kathy and Sally compiled all of the data and conducted lengthy sessions with both the executive team and the board, and we came up with a plan consisting of a mission, vision, institutional core values, core practices of our work, goals, strategies, and task assignments along with start and end dates. After months of work, we were proud to have produced a first-rate document. We owe a lot to Kathy and Sally for helping us produce an important component to our foundation and doing it in record time.

Another major project Kathy and Sally worked on was to develop a plan to help build a culture in our new organization. We had a unique opportunity to start from scratch and instill in all of our new employees a regard for the kind of atmosphere and interpersonal communications model that would help our vibrant new college develop into a great place for everyone to work. Our staff liaison with Hagler and Associates again was Cathy Hampton, who did an incredible job keeping things organized and prepared. Kathy Hagler also conducted board training.

One of the thornier issues we wrestled with was the selection of an employee benefits package. Cheryl did the research and found that even though we were not state employees, we could opt to join the state system because code provided that community colleges enjoyed that option. We had all been on the Public Employees Retirement System (PERSI) or state Optional Retirement Programs (ORPs) as BSU employees and were already familiar with them. We did compare them, however, to private companies offering similar benefits. We were convinced that joining the state system provided CWI employees the best coverage at the most economical rates, and I pushed for that package strongly with our board.

The Board of Trustees, though, struggled with the recommendation. They were torn between the options of giving a public entity our business versus a private local company. At their request, we all heard presentations from two private companies but it proved difficult to compare them to the state plan. The differences were subtle and the cost was hard to pin down mainly due to the fact that we had to predict how many employees we would have and their dates of hire over a period of several years in order to draw a valid comparison. The board finally voted and on a split decision, decided to go with the state system. I was delighted, personally, and believe to this day the right decision was made.

Two other major initiatives were chugging steadily along in the background during all of the more visible changes.

One was the preparation and actual transfer of the staff, faculty, and programs of the Selland College of Applied Technology from BSU. The other was the negotiation for properties so that CWI would remain accessible to students in both Ada and Canyon counties, and also be capable of housing the Selland College.

My role as president was to oversee all of these initiatives and to support individual team members as needed. I also kept busy putting out brushfires, making sure the desires of our Board were carried out and that we were making progress quickly enough in all areas. I also found myself up to my eyeballs in alligators helping some impatient people understand how complicated this whole adventure was and convincing them that things were progressing.

A part of my responsibility was to appear and testify before the Senate and House Education Committees as well as the

Joint Finance Appropriations Committee of the state legislature each year.

The legislators supported us and were eager to hear about our progress. Senator John Goedde, Chairman of the Education Committee, had been a long-time supporter. Just prior to the referendum, he wrote a guest opinion piece for the *Idaho Press-Tribune* on May 6, 2007 where he said "the Treasure Valley is on the verge of making history…for educational reasons, for economic development opportunities and for affordable access, I urge you to vote yes for the College of Western Idaho when you go to the polls May 22."

I was frequently on the guest speaker list for Chambers of Commerce and for numerous civic organizations around the valley. I met with mayors, county commissioners, and many other elected officials. My presentation became well polished and I was able to easily modify it to reflect progress. To say that there was considerable interest in the founding of the college is definitely an understatement.

As we progressed, we were trying to do many things simultaneously. It became quite complicated. In fact it grew so complicated and there were so many deadlines facing us, that we again hired Jerry Gee to help us with a written operational plan.

It resulted in an involved 67-page document with accompanying Gantt Charts designed to provide our staff and the Board of Trustees a listing of the crucial items that had to be digested and stamped "complete" along with deadlines for each and the person or persons responsible. It was divided into sections including finance, human resources, instruction, public relations, the foundation, governance, accreditation, student services, information technology, facilities, state board of education, state division of professional-technical education, and finally all other agencies both state and county having requirements for us.

The good news was that we were a blank slate and could create anything; the bad news was that we were a blank slate and had to start from scratch with no blueprint to follow.

Any organization would be challenged to take on formulating a new budget and business plan with no history to work from, or developing and implementing an accreditation strategy, or developing a detailed organizational structure, or developing branding (colors, logo, etc.), or developing a new marketing plan, or building the "business" of an organization, or developing all new policies and procedures, or developing all new systems and procedures, or developing a strategic plan, or adopting and implementing a salary and benefits package, or negotiating and contracting for several properties all at the same time, or "untangling" a 60-year-old technical college from a university and state system…whew. We were doing all of these things and many others concurrently along with learning, loading, and testing brand new computer software that none of us had any experience with.

My executive team met every week, from half a day to all day. The agenda called for the managers to summarize what they had accomplished during the past week and what they were working on for the current week. Each participant handled several things at once so their reports were always lengthy and involved. Even though every member of the team was chosen for his or her particular area of expertise, each one furnished feedback to the others and we all helped solve each others' problems.

The group dynamic was just that—dynamic—and I often marveled at the give and take and the openness to criticism and willingness to help that each member exhibited. All major decisions were made by the group even though the implementation of each decision usually fell to one individual.

Even though my team epitomized the concept of collegiality and participatory management, we were not immune from stress, which took its toll on us. I remember one particular time when two members of my team were having a real problem with each other and I finally had to address it. I called them in and worked through a mediation model I had used in my counseling days. I started out with a statement such as "I am only going to say this once; this will not continue… when you walk out the door this will be resolved one way or the other." Then I directed a structured, timed exchange between the two and we were able to get things worked out.

This kind of enmity was very rare and I can't think of words complimentary enough to describe how much the College of Western Idaho owes Victor, Cheryl, Brian, Shirl, Cathy, and Debbie and the wonderful people they hired along the way. None of these folks were constrained by a standard 40-hour work week. They worked tirelessly to lay all the groundwork for getting the doors open for credit classes in 16 months, an achievement that needs, and richly deserves to be, celebrated.

7 Instant Occupational Training

Most community colleges starting from scratch have to wait years to put in place funding, classrooms and labs, curriculum, equipment, approvals and the entire infrastructure necessary to start occupational training. Labs alone are capital intensive.

The College of Western Idaho had the luxury of being able to transfer the programs from an existing professional-technical college at Boise State University. While that was an exciting and unique opportunity, we soon found that the transfer would be exceedingly complicated and time consuming.

The Larry G. Selland College of Applied Technology (LSCAT) was the unit that provided professional-technical education and training for BSU and helped fulfill Boise State's community college mandate.

The Selland College has a long and rich history of its own.

LSCAT traces its origin to 1939 when a committee of nine was appointed to study the vocational needs for the newly established Boise Junior College. In school year 1939-40, Forestry and Secretarial Science were started, and that initiated a long history of service to the region. After World War II, a major renovation of airplane hangars was accomplished to house vocational programs on campus.

More programs were added in rapid succession during the 1950s and 60s, including Radio Technology, Woodworking, Auto Body, Machine Tool, Sheet Metal, Drafting, Practical Nursing, Welding, and Dental Assisting; Office Machine Repair, Data Processing, and Horticulture were soon added.

During the 1970s the first permanent instructional building was erected while more new programs started including Electrical Lineman, Plant Maintenance, Operating Room Technician, Child Care, Refrigeration, Heating and Air Conditioning, Diesel Mechanic, and Consumer Electronics to name a few. More permanent buildings followed, and soon there was a considerable structural and programmatic presence on the BSU campus.

Throughout the 1980s, '90s and well into the first decade of this century, there was a continual adding, tweaking, or suspension of programs to reflect the times and the educational and training needs of the workforce in the Treasure Valley. Guiding the ever-evolving college was an active College Advisory Committee comprised of community leaders as well as Technical Advisory Committees, consisting of industry experts, for every program.

The college functioned simply as a unit of Boise Junior College, but as the institution grew from BJC to Boise College in 1965, to Boise State College in 1969, and to Boise State University in 1974, LSCAT's designation and prominence changed as well.

In 1988, BSU initiated an engineering program and started a new unit called the College of Technology consisting of the School of Vocational-Technical Education and the School of Engineering. Dr. John Entorf became the first dean, and that was the year I went to work for the College of Technology, serving as a division manager supervising a number of vocational training programs as well as the director of the Canyon County Center in Nampa.

Dr. Entorf passed away within the first year of taking over and a national search was conducted for his replacement. I chaired that search, which selected Tom MacGregor who served as dean until 1997. Tom made a lasting impact on the new college. He brought energy, along with political and financial savvy to the position, and completely reorganized the College of Technology. He was instrumental in helping the new School of Engineering get off the ground and bringing the two schools together.

By that year, both schools within the College of Technology had grown to the point that BSU decided to make each a separate college. The new college designated to serve the vocational-technical training needs was named the Larry G. Selland College of Applied Technology, and Dr. Larry Barnhardt was appointed as the first dean. Dr. Barnhardt served for 10 years and retired. The last dean to serve prior to the transfer of the college to CWI was Dr. Vera McCrink.

Special recognition should be given to the late Larry Selland, as he was the reason for the new name of the college. Dr. Larry Selland came to Idaho in 1977 from North Dakota where he served as the Department Administrator for Vocational Education. He was a nationally recognized expert in his field and had served as the President of the National Association of State Directors.

As the Idaho State Administrator for Vocational-Technical Education, Dr. Selland was instrumental in changing the whole approach to the delivery of vocational-technical education. He brought in such things as Tech Prep, the concept of helping high school students develop career pathways, and academic subjects being taught with an applied approach where vocational education could be melded with traditional academic classes. He believed strongly that there should not be different standards for vocational-technical and academic courses. In fact Idaho, under his leadership, became a national leader in terms of the philosophy and delivery of vocational-technical education.

Dr. Selland served in that capacity for nine years and moved to Boise State as Dean of the School of Vocational-Technical Education in 1986 where he guided the program until 1988. At that time he was named Vice President for Academic Affairs at BSU until he was asked to be acting president of the university in 2002 between the presidency of Dr. John Kaiser and the hiring of Dr. Charles Ruch, who served just prior to Dr. Bob Kustra.

Tragically, Larry was diagnosed with cancer and retired much too early. He is remembered as a very compassionate man by all of us who knew him. He was one of the few educational leaders who could bridge the "great divide" between academic and vocational-technical education and enjoy the respect of everyone. When the State Board of Education decided to name the new college after him, his former colleagues and friends were thrilled and gratified. His name lives on at CWI, since one of the streets on the campus is named after him.

The 10 years that Dr. Barnhardt served as dean of the newly formed Larry G. Selland College of Applied Technology proved to be productive ones. He expanded the college's presence in the region and regularly revamped and tailored programs to meet the needs of skill training in the Treasure Valley.

He also worked tirelessly to launch a community college, and he reorganized his college leadership by adding several associate deans (for: instruction, student services, and workforce development, to name just a few) with responsibilities that they would assume if a community college were to come to fruition. He was determined to be ready if Boise State received the funding to start the community college.

Even before BSU leadership committed to promoting and starting a community college (since they believed it wouldn't get started any other way), Larry helped people in the community understand the need. He even asked a small group of people to study the options available to form a college. I was honored to be a member of that group.

As everyone looked forward to an eventual community college in some form, there were two schools of thought as to how it should be set up. One advocated that with the newly reorganized Selland College, all that would be needed was to add the general education/transfer academic programs and an instant community college would become a reality since the Selland College already had its own infrastructure such as student services, financial department, IT, etc.

The other advocated for creation of an entirely new unit, and the Selland College would simply join it and provide the professional-technical education component. Either way, the Selland College was ready.

The notable thing is that Dr. Barnhardt was instrumental in raising the university's interest and involvement, by helping the community see the need for a comprehensive community college as well as preparing the staff and faculty of his college no matter what form it took. He took the whole community college discussion to the next level.

In the two short years we were given to plan, the transfer of the Selland College was easily the most complicated issue we faced. It sounded easy at first—simply lift it out of BSU and plunk in down at CWI.

There were many hurdles.

The State Division for Professional Technical Education (SDPTE) was especially interested in this whole scenario because they are responsible for the funding and monitoring of all the professional technical education (PTE) in Idaho. Because of that involvement, they agreed to pay one-third of a consultant's fee to help us work through the deepening swamp. We again asked Dr. Jerry Gee to do that work; his expertise proved to be invaluable.

Since Boise State University was designated as the provider of PTE for Region III by the State Board of Education (SBOE), we applied to have that designation changed. After BSU agreed to the change, Dr. Mike Rush, then Director of SDPTE, wrote the document that went to the SBOE for approval.

After two formal presentations, they approved the transfer so that CWI would be designated as the provider of PTE for Region III consisting of the 10 southwestern counties of Idaho. It was a huge leap of faith on the part of both the SDPTE and the SBOE to approve the designation when we weren't even open for business. I really commend their trust in the progress we were making as we madly worked through the process.

Another big challenge was taking inventory of all the equipment, tools, and other assets listed on the books at BSU for the Selland programs. After 60 years, you can only imagine the amount of equipment, inventory, and supplies that had to be listed and accounted for in more than 30 programs. There was the inevitable sorting out what had been purchased with BSU general funds and what was purchased with PTE funds and there was definitely some confusion in various areas. Cheryl Wright's staff worked closely with the finance staff at BSU, spending a lot of time figuring it all out. We then hired a consulting firm to do the actual inventory which took several months. Eventually all parties were satisfied that there was a fair splitting of assets.

While the inventory was underway, we hired Dave Teater, a longtime education consultant, to guide us in planning space needs for the PTE programs. We knew we needed a plan in place to transition the programs off the Boise State campus over the next several years. Teater worked closely with Brian Currin to both develop space needs and to look at possible properties upon which to locate the transferred programs. Dave developed two documents—an Educational Specification Plan and a Facilities Utilization Plan— both detailed, lengthy, and very well done. They served us well for our planning purposes.

Once we established July 1, 2009, as the official transfer date for the Selland College, the in-depth and detailed planning gained speed. For a year we met monthly with all the interested parties gathered around the table. I euphemistically called it the "E-8 Summit."

Because the process was so complicated and meant we were dealing with transferring state personnel and assets to a non-state entity, there was a lot of interest in how things shook out. The "E-8" included Dr. Mike Rush, who by then had become the Executive Director of the State Board of Education; Ann Stephens, Administrator, and Kirk Dennis, Chief Fiscal Officer for SDPTE; Clete Edmuson from the governor's office; Dr. Jeff Fox, Vice President for Instruction at the College of Southern Idaho; and Dr. Jerry Gee. The delegation from BSU included Dr. Sona Andrews, Provost and Vice President for Academic Affairs; Stacy Pearson, Vice President, Finance and Administration; Dr. Vera McCrink, Dean of the Selland College; Kevin Satterlee, Associate Vice President and General Counsel and others as needed.

The CWI contingent consisted of Cheryl, Victor, Brian, and me as well as a Board of Trustees member (Mark Dunham was usually able to attend the meetings, but if not, M.C. Niland, Guy Hurlbutt, or Hatch Barrett attended). Also with our group was our legal counsel, Rich Stover. Dr. Andrews chaired the first half of the year, and I chaired the second half. Both delegations approached the meetings with sincerity and a desire to compromise. Given the incredible complexities we all faced as well as the sensitive nature of "un-entangling" millions of dollars in assets, that is saying a lot.

Both at the "E-8 Summit" and in dozens of other meetings, we encountered several roadblocks. These entanglements centered on such things as budgeting and financials, curriculum approvals and refinement, facilities and human resources.

Relative to the budget and finances, there was about $7.2 million in funding from the SDPTE that came with the transfer. The SBOE, through the SDPTE, finances the cost of instruction for professional-technical education throughout Idaho at both the secondary and post-secondary levels. The SDPTE also monitors the funds to ensure proper use, as well as approving all changes in PTE instruction.

There were numerous meetings with the SDPTE to iron out all the wrinkles. Ann Stephens, Administrator of SDPTE, was helpful and easy to work with. Her Chief Fiscal Officer, Kirk Dennis, was also good to work with, but expressed a lot of concerns about the transfer relative to making sure we would be in compliance since a lot of federal and state funds were at stake.

The discussions were complicated and lengthy. During one of our sessions, it was suggested that we would have to fire all Selland employees, then they would have to reapply for their jobs, a proposal which caused Victor Watson to declare that he would resign if that were to happen—I agreed to follow suit. We stood our ground and were able to work through the problem with the able assistance of Jerry Gee and Dick Ledington (with the SDPTE). This incident proved to be one of several lynch-pins we slugged our way through so that we could honor the promises made to both BSU and CWI.

Curriculum was a whole other matter. The issue became a bit complicated since the College of Southern Idaho (CSI) was our accreditation partner and would be until we received our own accreditation, something that could not happen overnight, and in fact would take several years. This partnership meant that we were essentially, for a time, a teaching location of CSI. It also meant that the entire Selland curriculum must line up with CSI's catalog, except that it didn't on all fronts.

In other words, all the programs that both institutions offered had to be the same, and the programs that CSI didn't offer must be accepted and shown in their catalog. Dr. Jerry Gee, our consultant, teamed up with Dr. Vera McCrink, Dean of Selland, and all her staff to coordinate details for the approvals at CSI. Dick Ledington at the SDPTE worked tirelessly and immersed himself in many meetings with Dr. Gee and staff from both Selland and CSI to work out all the bugs. Obviously, as I noted, everything had to be melded with the College of Southern Idaho, our accreditation partner. Dr. Jeff Fox, Vice President of Instruction, was the key person from the Twin Falls location and was great to work with.

Another curriculum stickler popped up in the area of nursing training. Selland College had a Licensed Practical Nursing program that didn't line up with the program at CSI. More meetings and negotiations shook out before that mountain was scaled. In addition, BSU's curriculum listed an Associate of Science (AS) Registered Nursing (RN) program that they intended to transfer to us via the Selland College. We wanted to change it to an Associate of Applied Science (AAS) RN program because PTE funding would pay the instructional costs. CSI refused to allow the change in degree designation. They already offered the AS, and they felt it was a more prestigious degree than the AAS even though the curriculum was essentially the same. The problem was that by doing what they asked, we would have to pay for the program from the general fund, and that could become a game-changer for us. We finally worked everything out with kudos to Cathleen Currie, our Nursing Department Chair, who negotiated tirelessly to push all the approvals through the State Board of Nursing – an extensive process. In essence, finally, we acquiesced to CSI: They were calling the shots in accreditation.

Still another thorny thicket grew around who would "teach out" the Selland students who were in two-year technical programs and would be transferred at the end of the first year.

BSU's position was that this was our problem and we would have the responsibility since the professional-technical programs were to be transferred to us. The problem was that the students had signed up for a certificate or degree from BSU. The real challenge was BSU convincing CSI that they should accept these students (since they were now our accreditation partner). CSI, however, had additional requirements if they were to take these students on—which of course violated the agreement that the students had signed when they enrolled at Selland College—a part of BSU.

You can see it really became a kind of three-ring circus. Jeff Fox, Vice President for Instruction at CSI, deserves a lot of credit here, because he worked through this log-jam with BSU and CWI with patience and professionalism even though at times the atmosphere was tense and stressful. CSI eventually agreed to allow us to take responsibility for these students and Jeff's staff and ours dealt with each student on an individual basis granting waivers where necessary.

The last, and probably the most difficult area to sort out, was easy to predict—personnel and all the changes of status that would necessarily result.

It was difficult from both a technical and emotional standpoint. From a technical viewpoint, as I have mentioned, transferring state employees to a non-state entity and having that transition take place in a smooth manner was doubly difficult. In the spring of 2008, the contract (primarily the instructional faculty and professional staff) Selland employees were told by BSU that the one-year contract under which they were working would be their last, and the non-contract employees (primarily classified hourly staff) were told that by June 30, 2009, they also would no longer be employed. There were about 125 people involved in the transfer, and they were, of course, filled with angst and had many questions about their future.

The changes affecting classified employees were the most challenging because those employees were part of the State of Idaho Employees System, and there were strict rules and regulations regarding them. They were given the option of transferring to CWI or remaining with BSU. If they decided to remain with BSU, they were given three chances to turn down available openings. If they turned down all three, they would be terminated. Also as part of the deal, BSU was obligated to hire them if they chose one of the openings.

Boise State University's Office of Human Resources offered assistance to all the Selland employees during this gut-check experience. Jane Buser and her staff, particularly Debi Alvord, were instrumental in the change-over. Debi even prepared a binder listing all the procedures, steps, and timelines for the professional and classified employees. They also hired a staff person to work with the Selland personnel.

Due to the timing of the transfer, the issue of funding a looming gap in salaries developed for many of the people. SDPTE stepped up and covered those expenses. But for a time there was a lot of anguish as to how such a chasm could be bridged.

The human, emotional aspect of all these changes predictably proved to be the toughest on everyone. One can only imagine how the Selland employees felt when they were told that they must involuntarily leave the university (where many had worked for years) and the state system of benefits, and go to CWI, not knowing what to expect. I suppose it is much like what happens in the private sector with mergers and takeovers. For most of a year these men and women were left hanging until we could provide answers to their most pressing questions directed to our Board of Trustees. Dr. Sona Andrews, from BSU, met regularly with them and tried to answer their questions, but of course, she had little direct knowledge of our situation.

The Selland faculty approached us early on, wanting to be part of the planning process and to be involved in decision-making concerning instruction, but we were unable to respond because we were buried in work getting ready to open our doors to the first students for the spring, 2009 semester. On top of that, they were technically still BSU employees, and there were questions about how much we could solicit their involvement until they actually worked for us.

Our trustees fielded some very difficult questions flowing from the Selland group. I pushed for decisions from the board so I could provide answers to Selland employees' questions, as they pondered whether they were doing the right thing. The board did an amazing job considering what little first-hand knowledge they had of any of the issues. They scrambled to become informed and deal with the pressure I was piling on them for decisions as well as pressure they felt from the outside. By outside, I mean Selland advocates and the press who picked up on their concerns and published several articles concerning their anxiety.

The board and I had to wrestle with five major areas. First of all we questioned whether we should bring all the programs over as they existed or pick and choose selected programs. Unsolicited advice favored picking and choosing. I argued that to do so, we would not get all the $7.2 million that came with the transfer to cover the instructional costs. I felt that once we delivered the transfer alive and breathing, or kicking and screaming as the case may be, we could decide which programs we would keep, and then we could reallocate funds from suspended programs to other programs. Another issue hovered. Should we opt to pick and choose, we would have difficulty unilaterally closing several programs since the SDPTE had final say and, of course, held the purse strings. The board voted to bring all the programs over, but was concerned with faculty salaries appearing to be much higher than what we were paying our general education/transfer faculty. They stipulated that a salary study be conducted during the first year under CWI and possible adjustments be made. As a result of the board's direction, all subsequent PTE faculty brought on during our administration were hired at salaries more in line with our general education faculty until the salary study could occur.

The second major decision point loomed over whether the non-faculty Selland employees should be brought over in their current positions along with salaries. I think there was a feeling among some board members that we ought to scale back staff (professional and classified) and adjust salaries. Again, I argued that we leave everything unchanged for the same reasons I had given them. The board agreed.

A third and very prickly cactus was deciding whether we would stay with the current state system for health, life, dental, disability, insurance etc. or design another package and purchase it from a private vendor. As I stated before, state code allows community colleges to opt into the state system even though we aren't a state agency. Our Board of Trustees really struggled with this one and finally did accept my recommendation but the decision was not unanimous.

A fourth crucial decision they had to make concerned whether our employees should stay in the state system for retirement. All of the Selland employees, as well as those of us already a part of CWI, were either in the state PERSI system or in a state-sponsored Optional Retirement Program. A lot was riding on this decision for all of us; I urged the board to continue under that arrangement. Thankfully, they agreed.

The next major decision I asked from the board dealt with the transfer of earned vacation and sick leave. The transfer of earned vacation was especially troublesome because it represented a potential liability of more than $485,000 that CWI would assume. The problem is that if an employee was fired or resigned, CWI would be obligated to pay for all the unused vacation days. Normally, people take vacations and there is no liability issue, but if enough people were allowed to build up vacation days and in the very unlikely event they were all to quit at the same time, a financial crisis could conceivably result. I argued that the liability was really only "on paper" since the odds of a large group quitting in mass was remote and with what all the Selland folks were going through, it was the right thing to do.

The sick leave issue was a problem because state code didn't allow the transfer of accumulated sick leave from a state entity to a non-state entity. Governor Otter entered the mix and the SDPTE wrote a bill which was approved by the legislature to temporarily change the code.

Our Board of Trustees had no qualms approving it, and after several months they also approved the transfer of unused vacation leave.

C. L. "BUTCH" OTTER
GOVERNOR

May 16, 2008

Dear Selland College Employee,

As you probably know, the Larry G. Selland College of Applied Technology soon will be transferred from Boise State University to the College of Western Idaho. It is my understanding that Boise State University, the Idaho State Board of Education, and College of Western Idaho expect that Selland College will transfer all its property, students, faculty and staff to the College of Western Idaho. When that happens, Selland College will cease being a part of state government and its employees no longer will be employed by the state.

I understand that one of the concerns some of you have about your potential move to the College of Western Idaho is the possibility that your unused PERSI sick leave will be forfeited. I have been advised that PERSI does not believe it currently has the authority to transfer your unused sick leave from Boise State University to the College of Western Idaho.

You should not be penalized by the College of Western Idaho's assumption of community college functions in southwestern Idaho. Please rest assured that my office will work with PERSI and with the Legislature to prevent the loss of unused sick leave if you move to the College of Western Idaho.

The opening of the College of Western Idaho is an important step for education in southwestern Idaho. I am committed to ensuring the employees of Selland College maintain the benefits they have earned while serving the State of Idaho.

As Always – Idaho, "Esto Perpetua"

C.L. "Butch" Otter
Governor of Idaho

Governor Otter intervenes

During all this time, the Selland College staff and faculty felt the CWI administration was not really responding to their questions, and they were feeling, to say the least, anxious about the whole transfer. We were just as frustrated because we couldn't provide answers when they needed them. Eventually everything cooled down, the dust settled and as the school year 2008-2009 arrived, we all had a much clearer view of the future.

Dr. Melanie Reese, who was on the Selland staff and is a mediation expert, deserves some special recognition. She worked effectively to keep the lines of communication open between my staff, the Selland staff and faculty. Cathy Hampton was also effective in working to help both the Selland College personnel and my executive staff understand the issues on both sides and to help us fashion solutions.

Dr. Vera McCrink, who found herself in the difficult position of having to keep the Selland College operating in a sort of "lame duck" fashion the year before the transition and also having to act as the "go-between" for Selland and CWI, deserves recognition. She did a terrific job in a very, very tough situation. She and her center managers, Mike Lyons, Sue Madarieta, Cathleen Currie, Jeff Schroeder, and Susan Johnson all stepped up and worked under difficult conditions with their people.

Many issues were negotiated with Boise State and the Selland College, but I hope I have given the reader enough so as not to inundate, but to present examples of the complexities we faced.

The Selland College was a wonderful addition and completed us in our quest to become a comprehensive community college as quickly as possible.

We now had more than 30 credit-earning certificate/degree occupational programs, a sizable workforce development/business partnerships department offering short-term, non credit, job related classes to companies both at their sites and in our classrooms, and a significant Apprenticeship Program where working people in the trades could qualify to become journeymen in several fields. In addition, we managed Adult Basic Education classes over the 10 counties of southwest Idaho that included tutoring, English as a Second Language Program, and helped hundreds of students prepare for and take their GED Exams.

8 The Facilities Challenge

While the transfer of the Selland College programs proved to be more than challenging, another project going on at the same time also fueled the furnace of our stress level during the formation of the College of Western Idaho. Logistically, we were confronted with providing classroom and lab facilities for the students along with finding administrative space to support students and staff. The other obstacle was to construct this entire framework in a way that would distribute fair if not entirely equal access to the college over the two-county area.

Most community colleges start by offering classes at night in facilities such as local high schools, and it literally takes years to purchase and develop property and find funding for buildings. What happened for us seems astounding. We inherited a developed campus with a beautiful near-new classroom building along with a second campus with yet another first-class classroom building.

Even though this was a phenomenal development, it, like everything else, proved to be extremely challenging in many ways.

To describe what happened, I have to refer back to Dr. Bob Kustra, President of Boise State University.

As I discussed earlier, he worked tirelessly to help the community and the legislature understand the importance of establishing a comprehensive community college in the valley.

When it appeared that effort, along with everything else previously described, wasn't getting any traction with the Idaho Legislature, Bob decided to try to start a community college as a separate college within Boise State University with the idea of spinning it off at a later date. During many public presentations, he mentioned that he would commit the BSU West Campus to the community college, and in fact the "Community College Yes" campaign began to use that as one of its major points to gain voter support in the pending referendum.

Then as the referendum campaign gathered momentum, Kustra reiterated that the West Campus could be the community college campus—in fact he was quoted several times as saying (and I'm paraphrasing) "I have never had such a hard time giving something away in my life." I am convinced he was sincere, but with the unspoken or unreported understanding that BSU be held harmless financially both in the loss of property and buildings, and in the loss of potential students to CWI.

At any rate, after the referendum passed and the new CWI Board of Trustees was elected, the pressure on Bob to fulfill his "promise" mounted. CWI Board Chairman Jerry Hess designated trustees Mark Dunham and Guy Hurlbutt to work on the transfer of BSU's West Campus to CWI, and our board wasn't thinking in terms of reimbursement to BSU. Both Mark and Guy put an enormous amount of intense work into this transfer; we are more than grateful for all they did. We would not have launched two campuses with 21st century teaching facilities had it not been for Mark and Guy's talent and dedication.

Jerry could not have chosen two more qualified people to negotiate the property transfer. Mark wanted to be on the sub-committee because he had worked for the Idaho Association of Commerce and Industry which had been instrumental in driving the support for the community college. He had also worked for Boise State, specifically for Bob Kustra, and developed a strong relationship with the State Board of Education. Guy is well respected in the community with ties to key players. He is also a retired attorney, who turned out to be helpful in understanding the constant revisions and various versions of what ultimately became the contract.

Both Guy and Mark described the negotiations as being collegial and respectful and much of the process was handled at "arms' length" through phone calls and e-mails. The President of the State Board of Education, Milford Terrell, chose Board Member Rod Lewis to represent him and his colleagues. Milford, nevertheless, became deeply involved personally.

The process began in December 2007, and ran through the spring of 2008. The negotiators spent countless hours working on the project with much of the effort occurring after regular work hours and on weekends. Guy even committed several hours while on vacation in Hawaii, as he described it "on a phone under a palm tree."

There was much ground to plow. One of the first trouble spots that had to be worked out was the requirement that under Idaho code, state owned property could not be given to a non-state entity. Under then State Senator Brad Little's leadership, the Legislature granted a waiver of that portion of the code.

Brad Little now serves as the lieutenant governor of Idaho. He was instrumental during the time he served as a state senator and he was a major driver of the whole effort to get the initiative passed. Senator Little was the one state legislator from the western part of the valley who consistently came to rallies, gave speeches in support of the need for a community college, talked to key leaders to get their backing, and did heavy lifting in a myriad of other ways.

His legislative expertise and help with all the complications that arose as we negotiated the transfer of the Selland College and the transfer of the properties from BSU to us was crucial to making it all work. We owe him a debt of gratitude.

Another stumbling block involved the fact that the land was owned by the State Board of Education and the building was owned by the State Building Authority which was handling the bonds that had been sold under the State of Idaho to finance it. So there had to be separate talks with the Building Authority. It was a complicated process and we all owe a huge debt of gratitude to Wayne Meuleman and Dick Mollerup, legal partners, who did all of the title work for free. The result was a legal document five inches thick. While I'm passing out kudos to attorneys, our legal counsel Rich Stover, not only worked hard and competently in this process but also handled dozens of other legal issues for us at the same time.

The most imposing land mine was to determine how to divide the 150-acre parcel known as the BSU West Campus, along with the buildings already on it. The State Board and BSU maintained early on in the discussion that they should keep part of the property because one of the buildings, the Technology and Entrepreneurial Center (TEC), was paid for through a grant from the Economic Development Administration and was functioning successfully. In addition, both the university and the state board of education sought to eventually have a facility adjacent to CWI for the ease of students who wanted to transition after completing two years. The proposed property solutions varied from all of it going to CWI, to splitting it 50/50, or splitting it by some other percentage.

After much wrangling, it was decided that the plot would be divided so the state board of education retained 50 acres along with the TEC Center and CWI received 100 acres and the new academic building. After additional negotiations, the federal Economic Development Administration granted permission for division of the property.

After deciding what the split would be, drawing boundaries posed another quandary. Sometimes historic and lasting decisions are made in a very informal and personal way. One hot afternoon Milford Terrell met Guy, Mark, and our attorney, Rich, on the property and literally walked much of the area talking and questioning "what about this or that." They finally came to a decision on where to put the boundaries. It might seem to some as a rather inelegant way to arrive at such a monumental decision, but it proved effective.

Main Campus Property

(Courtesy of CWI)

Along with the issue of the BSU West property was the question concerning the BSU Canyon County Center (an additional five-acre campus on Nampa-Caldwell Boulevard), and the transfer of it also loomed large. The negotiators ultimately decided that both BSU satellite campuses would become part of CWI. I have to admit that both the 77,000 square-foot structure at the Canyon County Center and the 65,000 square-foot building on BSU's West Campus were well equipped educational sites, and both buildings were nearly new. Since BSU had paid, from their general funds, to furnish and equip both buildings a decision also had to be made as to how much we were to reimburse them. As it turned out, the BSU administration was fair in the amount they wanted to be paid, and I have to thank Stacy Pearson, BSU's Vice President for Finance and Administration, who couldn't have been easier to work with and couldn't have been more reasonable.

Ultimately, the campus question sifted down to an understood quid pro quo arrangement whereby we would be given the two campuses and buildings if we took on the entire Selland College, freeing BSU to pursue its dream of evolving into a metropolitan research university. The initial agreement also required CWI to take all the employees at their current salaries. As I mentioned, our Board agreed to that arrangement with the stipulation that all programs and salaries would be reviewed within the first year of the transfer. In return for the property and facilities, CWI agreed to a date certain to lift all the programs off the BSU Campus (three years hence) and vacate 32,000 square-feet of classroom and office space from BSU's campus by July 1, 2009, followed by removal of the remainder by July 1, 2012.

Arriving at the agreed upon figure of 32,000 square-feet to be freed up on the BSU campus was a difficult process. During negotiations with the State Board, Mark Dunham called me one day and asked how much space we could open up for BSU by July 2009, and he wanted an answer virtually at once. We began to scramble and with the hard work of Brian Currin and Cathy Hampton, we came up with a plan to move the Selland College completely out of the Engineering Technology Building and clear out the entire first floor of the Technical Services Building on the BSU campus. There had been increasing pressure for some time from the Engineering College to acquire full use of their building.

I made it clear to Mark that we had no place to put the transplanted programs and supporting personnel or the funds to move them and that we would need financial help to pull all of that off. Apparently, however, the State Board and BSU were supportive of our proposal so the deal was struck.

There were, predictably when dealing with academics and politics, other more subtle kinds of issues permeating the entire process. For example, the land for BSU West had been originally donated to BSU with the stipulation that it would be sold and the money spent on athletics. Under former BSU President Charles Ruch, a university branch campus was created instead. Then when President Bob Kustra came to BSU, he pushed for the land to become a community college campus. This entire political undercurrent created angst among many people in the western part of the valley who felt they had been handed a string of broken promises. The pressure cooker of history created all the more steam in the negotiation process. I was involved in all of these changes, as the public face for BSU in Canyon County, and had to deal with the public relations ramifications. The atmosphere boiled into occasional thunder storms. Mark Dunham felt similar pressure in his legislative dealings.

A short note about the facilities that were transferred to CWI: In my role with Boise State, I was on the design team which constructed the new building on the Canyon County Center site and the remodel of the existing building, both of which were completed by 2003. They were well-equipped, state-of-the-art facilities.

Funding for the Canyon County Center addition and remodel, the West Campus purchase and the infrastructure at the West Campus came directly from the State Legislature with special thanks going to then Senators Atwell Perry and Jerry Thorne who worked hard to obtain the construction funding. Both senators were from Canyon County and had long since retired when the final push for CWI got underway. I knew them well and would see Jerry Thorne at Rotary every week. The legacy they both left regarding a significant educational presence in the western part of the valley by establishing BSU there is hugely significant. They have both passed and I miss them.

On the main campus, the BSU West Campus building is truly a 21st century facility and the property it sits on is prime real estate. Work on the campus began in 2001 when the legislature allocated $5 million to develop the 150 acres. A framework campus master plan was completed with supporting infrastructure to develop about 50 acres of the property. That infrastructure included streets, curbs, streetlights, and landscaping. It also included underground data, electric lines, water, sewer, and a sprinkler system. A bridge also was built over the canal running across campus. In 2003, the legislature decided to sell bonds and build a classroom facility for BSU on that site as part of a bill that included new buildings on all the campuses of Idaho's colleges and universities.

In 2005, we opened the doors of a beautiful and functional building. It had state-of-the-art chemistry and biology labs along with a variety of classrooms as well as two first-class computer labs. A bookstore, faculty offices, and a student support services suite were also part of the facility. Again, in my role with BSU, I served on the design team and had the added responsibility of equipping the building for faculty and students. Along with the hard work of Management Assistant Debbie Jensen, we opened the building on time and on budget. I was gratified by what we were able to do and then to have it become the first building for the new community college, with me serving as president, was almost more than I could have imagined.

Transferring all of the property and buildings was not without cost in terms of people's feelings and attitudes toward us.

An example of that was expressed loud and clear when our attorney Rich Stover and I went before the Idaho State Board of Education to get preliminary approval for the transfer. Rich spent countless hours working with both the BSU and State Board attorneys to draft the final documents and they all signed off that everything was in place.

President of the State Board, at the time, Milford Terrell, had been contrarily advised, because he took us to task in a very direct and confrontational way. Understand that Milford is a very large, physically imposing man who seems bigger than life. When he comes into a room, he tends to take it over. He has a loud booming voice and when he is upset, there is no doubt in anyone's mind.

There were a tense few moments for both Rich and me.

Terrell's problem resulted from his belief that the contract didn't sufficiently guarantee BSU ingress and egress to their 50 acres. Rich tried to explain that question had been handled in a separate document, all of which had been previously agreed upon by the three attorneys. Milford apparently wasn't buying any of it. I was told later that he was motivated in part because he felt BSU got the short end of the stick and that we weren't appreciative enough of their sacrifice. Whatever the motivation, it was obvious that there were bruised feelings, not only Terrell's, but also many who supported BSU.

The whole incident was blown further out of proportion, becoming even more awkward when Bob Kustra, in front of the board, presented me with a huge painting of the West Campus with a bow and ribbon tied around it as a token of his good faith regarding the transfer, and in his remarks said jokingly that we were welcome to the gift in the amount written on the back of the painting ($43 million). I responded to him and the board that CWI was very appreciative of both the property and of BSU's partnership throughout these changes. I also said that the first thing I was going to do was to have the painting touched up with the routes of egress and ingress clearly marked in orange and blue (BSU's colors). It got a laugh and the tension eased… perhaps a degree or two. To Milford's credit, he apologized to me after the meeting. I have great respect for him and what he has done for education in Idaho.

Rich and I met again the next week with the State Board where they were holding a short meeting via conference call and the action was ratified. Several months later final approval came at a regular meeting of the board. It was a tremendous relief for me. It also proved to be the last time I would formally meet with them prior to my retirement. They did, however, invite me to one final meeting in August 2009, where they were gracious in their praise for what we had accomplished and presented me with a plaque. I was pleased that we were able to work everything out.

We concluded with an amazing gift, and I challenge anyone to find a college start-up anywhere in the country with two facilities as modern and as functional along with two campuses with which to start a community college.

College of Western Idaho was extremely fortunate and I credit much to Milford Terrell and Rod Lewis of the State Board of Education and to Dr. Bob Kustra and his staff at BSU. Huge thanks also go to Guy Hurlbutt and Mark Dunham who worked long and hard to make all this happen. The faculty, staff, and most of all the students, owe these folks a debt of gratitude.

"It's official"

(Courtesy of CWI)

Once the facilities transfer took place, we had more logistics work to do to actually occupy the former BSU West Campus Building. CWI had little time to transition the building from BSU because their fall, 2008 semester ended and three weeks later CWI started its first semester of classes. Brian Currin had his hands full dealing with a host of facility remodeling and upgrading including changing signage throughout the building, replacing all locks and installing a new keying system. On top of that, all the mechanical maintenance contracts had to be re-negotiated (HVAC, elevators, etc.). Tom Herseth, a BSU Facilities Supervisor, played a key role in helping Brian get the building refitted. In addition to the facilities plan, Brian was also responsible for Information Technology such as implementing a new phone system, changing out the network connections, and moving all PCs and printers onto the new network.

After Brian and his staff got the former BSU West Campus Building operational for classes in record time, he had to get the Canyon County Center ready for us to occupy by fall 2009. Again he faced similar issues to those just outlined in getting the building turned over from BSU. In addition, he addressed several needed maintenance tasks including replacing carpeting with vinyl flooring in the common areas, new paint throughout the building, and renovating the restrooms.

Since the BSU West Campus Building was originally designed as a satellite teaching facility, it didn't come close to having the space required for a full college's administrative offices. Brian negotiated a great deal involving a new office complex building called Aspen Creek right across the street. The developer was Dave Evans who was amenable to our plans. He wanted CWI to be the anchor tenant and we were able to work out a deal that included six months free rent along with a desirable lease rate. Brian walked us through the design process and we were able to build it out to fit our needs.

Finding space to accommodate the programs and administrative personnel being displaced by the requirement to free up 32,000 square-feet from the BSU campus presented another huge facilities challenge. As I have already noted we had hired a consultant, Dave Teater, to help determine what facilities were needed to transfer all the Selland programs off the BSU campus to another location. As a result of Teater's excellent work, his study was used throughout the transfer process.

In conjunction with the transition, I decided early on (and the board agreed) that we needed to have a significant presence in Ada County. A higher percentage of the tax dollars to support CWI came from Ada County, and people toward the eastern edge of the valley needed easier access to student services support and classrooms than driving to Nampa. I envisioned being able to set up an Ada County Center, to go along with our new Canyon County Center, both anchored by the main campus (the former BSU West site).

To bring all this to fruition, Brian contracted with Colliers International to serve as our real estate broker and they showed us several properties in Ada County. We finally settled on the Pintail Center owned by the Sundance Corporation on the corner of Maple Grove and Overland in Boise. It encompassed 52,000 square-feet and allowed plenty of room for the transferred Selland programs and administrative offices as well as general education classrooms, a testing center, student services offices and a bookstore. However, negotiations proved to be grueling. Even though the building was just an empty shell and we would be able to design it from scratch to meet our exact needs, one of the sticky problems was how we were going to finance the $1.2 million in tenant improvements to cover the cost of the build-out. The only way we could pay for it was to roll the costs into our lease payment which the owner (the Sundance Corporation) was willing to do if we would commit to a long-term lease and if we could get out from under the "non-appropriation clause." The clause is embedded in the state constitution and reads in effect that a public entity, should public financial support stop, could be released from any financial obligations. That clause in the state statute became a major stumbling block until the J.A. and Kathryn Albertson Foundation agreed to underwrite the $1.2 million should something happen. Once more, the foundation came through with flying colors for education in southwest Idaho.

Negotiations went on and on over a variety of other peripheral issues and finally time began to run out. We needed to have the building ready in time for the Selland group to set up labs and have everything else installed and working for the fall 2009 semester.

Brian Currin and our broker were struggling to finalize the deal, and as I analyzed the time the owner said it would take him to retrofit the building and the time we needed to occupy the building, it became apparent that we were simply at a point of no return. I swallowed and decided to "pull the plug" on the project and ran it by our board chairman, Guy Hurlbutt, who agreed. I immediately sat down with Brian and told him to meet with our broker to let him know that time had run out.

Later that same morning, I got a call from the Sundance Corporation asking that we meet one more time. They seemed to express a new sense of urgency and since the negotiations were so knotted up and time was of the essence, I felt it important that a board member join us. Guy was out of town, so I asked Stan Bastian to join Brian and me for lunch with the Sundance principals. The meeting went smoothly and the owners not only agreed to accept responsibility to resolve the remaining impasse, but also offered additional caveats such as free storage during the move and additional workers to meet the deadline. We soon ironed out a contract and struck a deal. Work started immediately on the building and Brian began to work closely with the Dean and the Center Managers of the affected Selland programs, our student services personnel, as well as with the contractor to make sure the retrofitting met specifications.

At Colliers, Jeff Needs and Lew Manglos worked hard on our behalf. I must also thank Franklin Lee and Judson Montgomery at Givens Pursley who were essential in providing top-notch legal work.

For the fall semester 2009, residents of Ada County could now go to the new center to register for CWI classes, do any placement testing required, and buy books for classes no matter what location they were matriculating to. There were now, in addition, a variety of professional-technical programs in Business and in Information Technology as well as many general education classes available.

As a result of the agreement with the State Board requiring us to free up 32,000 square-feet of space at BSU right away, we had to deal with other entities besides the Business and IT programs, administrative offices, and student services. We had to find space for the Drafting, Nursing, and the Workforce Development Program (the short-term, non-credit, job related) arm of the Selland College. We decided to move Drafting to the Canyon County Center along with Nursing. Workforce Development presented a more formidable problem.

The Workforce Development Program, under the Selland College, was located on three different sites—the BSU main campus, a rented space on Bank Drive in Boise, and another rented facility on Vista Avenue (Oak Park Building) in Boise. Brian negotiated with brokers and Dave Teater to resolve our options and ultimately recommended that we end our lease at Bank Drive, and expand our presence at Oak Park where we could consolidate the Workforce Training Program. Brian also directed the retrofitting of the Oak Park location, which occurred at the same time as the build-out project at Pintail.

He had a lot on his plate!

As a result of the contract with the State Board, the remaining Selland programs could remain on the BSU Campus until 2012. We had to negotiate a lease with Boise State, and were able to work out a favorable rate. The caveat required that at the end of 2012, if we had any remaining programs on the BSU Campus, the rate would increase substantially.

Along with the Selland transfer came two other programs located on additional leased property: the Professional Truck Driving Program and the Horticulture Program. In both cases the lease agreements had to be rewritten and signed off by all parties.

By the spring of 2009, the College of Western Idaho facilities consisted of:

■ The Main Campus (the old BSU West Campus) in Nampa

■ The Canyon County Center in Nampa

■The Ada County Center in Boise

■ The Administrative Offices at Aspen Creek in Nampa

■ The Oak Park Center in Boise

■ A presence on the BSU Campus

■The Horticulture Program Site at the Idaho Botanical Gardens

■ The Professional Truck Driving facility in Nampa

Main Campus

Canyon County Center

Ada County Center

Administrative Offices

Oak Park Center

BSU Location

Horticulture Location

**Professional Truck Driving Location –
CWI Truck Driving Tractors**

(all location photos courtesy of CWI)

In addition to coordinating all of these projects—all happening at the same time—Brian was responsible for making sure that all locations had the proper signage (inside and out) and were connected by data and phones. He also had to ensure that they were all set up with custodial, maintenance, security, and mail services.

CWI owes him a debt of gratitude.

So rather than starting out as most community colleges do, in less than two years we began with a multi-campus, two-county operation. We added a new dimension to the phrase, "hit the ground running."

9 It All Pays Off

All of the twists and turns and hard work I have described in the previous chapters only tell part of a complicated story. I would bore the reader to tears if I presented more detail than I already have or if I replowed other ground that challenged us. As we worked through all the issues we knew there would be a payoff.

As professional educators we celebrated the payoff in a number of ways. The most gratifying was the day we were able to actually start teaching students. We got an early start by contracting with the Selland College and BSU to offer the Workforce Training classes under our marketing brand and our control in January 2008 (only five months after we came together as a team) even though the Selland College would not be officially transferred until July 2009. With this arrangement, we were able to show the public that we were making progress and were accepting students. Workforce Training served more than 12,000 people that year.

The payoff also occurred when I stood before the Idaho Legislative Joint Finance Appropriations Committee, the Senate Education Committee, and the House Education Committee in both January 2008 and 2009 to report on our progress where, despite lots of questions, the legislators seemed genuinely pleased.

The payoff was apparent when I spoke to dozens of civic and community organizations and radio and television stations throughout the two years outlining our progress. People in general seemed to be intensely interested in the community college becoming a success. It was heartwarming to talk with them after the meetings and realize how excited they were to become part of the new institution either as students or by sending their children there.

We started our first credit/transfer students in January 2009. We had originally planned to start these students in the fall of 2008, but we simply weren't ready. The main problem was that because we switched accreditation partners, it took longer to obtain the approval from our accrediting body, and without such an endorsement we couldn't offer federal financial aid. The approval finally came through only a few months before school started in January.

Our marketing campaign was ready to go as soon as accreditation approval was announced. Since we had such a short time to get students signed up, the campaign was aggressive. Not only was there very little time to get the word out before classes started, but we also faced the initial challenge of getting our identity out there. The valley is awash with commercial advertising urging people to sign up for every kind of educational program and training imaginable. We were faced with the reality that the University of Idaho, Idaho State University, Boise State University, Northwest Nazarene University, The College of Idaho, University of Phoenix, George Fox University and dozens of proprietary colleges (Stevens-Henagar College, Brown Mackey College, Apollo College, ITT, etc.) were all competing for students.

Our ad campaign involved imitating a popular TV commercial featuring two actors representing a Mac and a PC trying to one-up each other with the Mac always looking better. In our commercials, two actors would stand before the camera and one would say "I am the university" and the other would say "I'm the College of Western Idaho" and then the university actor would say something like, "Students should come to my institution because it offers a variety of degrees." The CWI actor would then say, "Students should come to my school because they can get a variety of degrees as well but at half the price."

Some critics in the community felt we were unfairly targeting BSU even though no institutions were named and there are, in fact, two other public and three private universities operating in the Treasure Valley.

Bob Kustra was especially upset over our advertising and made his feelings known in writing to the state board. In addition, he talked with one member of our board and stressed that "after all he and BSU had done to get CWI up and running, how could we treat them that way." The whole incident wasn't soon forgotten because when our second board chairman met with him, Bob again brought the issue up.

Looking back I certainly understand why he might feel that way, but we sincerely didn't believe we were attacking BSU or any other university in particular. Bob should have had more confidence in the powerful presence of his institution. In fact there are several examples of community colleges across the country starting in an area with an established university. In every case, not only does the community college flourish, but so does the university.

Whether or not the general public approved of our advertising approach (and several did not), it was effective—the registrations started pouring in. Our student services department worked long hours to handle the onslaught. They dealt with large numbers of prospective students while working out the inevitable kinks that tie-up any new operation. Dean Terry Blom and all his people deserve so much credit.

Courtesy of CWI

Another huge payoff occurred when we hosted our grand opening and ribbon cutting in mid-January 2009 just a week or so ahead of the start of classes. I had the honor of serving as master of ceremonies and was able to give a short speech even though our main speaker was Governor Otter. Board Chairman Guy Hurlbutt also spoke. The affair was attended by several hundred people and enjoyed comprehensive press coverage. The excitement and anticipation was evident among all those attending.

Governor Otter at grand opening

(Courtesy of CWI)

Chairman Hurlbut at grand opening

(Courtesy of CWI)

Speaking of the press, one experience stands out. They were, for the most part, supportive and helpful in keeping the public informed regarding our progress.

However, just prior to opening, reporters and broadcasters kept asking about a prediction of how many students we would start, but I was reluctant to give a number estimate because this was all new territory for us with no history to rely on.

Finally, one reporter asked me how many students had we had budgeted for, and I replied 1,700. That, predictably, became the benchmark the newspapers and all the TV stations used. When we finally started 1,208 students, the newspaper headlines and T.V. stories were variations of "CWI misses enrollment predictions."

One of the most frustrating examples of my many experiences during this "media feeding frenzy" was when one of the local TV stations called and asked for a comment about the "missed projection."

I explained that we had to pick a number for budget purposes with no history to rely on and that while we didn't make the 1,700 figure we had budgeted for, more than 1,200 students matriculated with us. Having only a little more than one month to advertise an institution which was brand new, with no identity or performance history, that number seemed to me to be more than acceptable. He replied that he would like to come out and do a story to explain our side of the issue.

He and his camera crew came out and took some pictures of empty classrooms (BSU still occupied the building and was out on Christmas vacation) and led the story that evening with guess what—"CWI missed their projection" again implying that CWI might be in trouble or that there might not be as much interest in students attending as many people thought.

This all turned out to be a burr under my saddle because there was certainly no script to follow and I knew compared to the way most community colleges start, 1,208 students was a more than acceptable way to launch the school especially when you consider we started in the middle of a school year.

Me before the press

(Courtesy of CWI)

To give you some perspective as to what we accomplished compared to other recent startups in the Northwest, let me share the following relative to their progress and their accreditation status.

Columbia Gorge Community College is still in candidate status after operating since 1989.

Tillamook Bay Community College is still in candidate status (awarded in 1989) after starting in 1984.

Cascadia Community College existed for four years before they offered their first class.

We had everything in place offering classes with an accreditation partner and were in the process of gaining candidacy which should happen in 2012. Full accreditation should occur around 2015-2016.

We established a community college in an urban area with a vibrant university already in place where there was the inevitable competition for lower division students; we had to transfer an entire college out of BSU and the state system, one already offering AA degrees and certificates; we had to do so working with an accreditation partner 150 miles away while operating under two completely different computer systems.

Another minor irritant to me was when we prepared our 2009 budget which had not yet been approved by the board; one of the local newspapers took a few of the line items out and published them in a headline questioning our judgment. One of the line items was for the purchase of some golf carts and the press and the article had a field day with that one. Never mind the fact that our administrative offices were probably three quarters of a mile from the main teaching building and that people had to cross a major highway to get back and forth. We thought the golf carts would be an inexpensive way to ferry the many people between locations.

We, did however, take the item out of the budget because it seemed easier than dealing with people's perceptions which often become reality.

Let me also say that for the most part, both television and newspaper reporters treated us fairly. I am grateful for the coverage from all our local TV channels, 2, 6, 7, and 12. Mike Butts with the *Idaho Press-Tribune* and Bill Roberts of the *Idaho Statesman* were both careful about checking facts and being thorough in their reporting. I spent many hours with each of them concerning various stories they were writing.

The payoff continued when I gave the first State of the College Address to all staff and faculty in early January 2009, just before we started offering our first credit/transfer classes to the public. The theme for my speech was that they were all pioneers and a part of something truly historic, something for which they would be remembered for a long time. In fact every employee was given a certificate naming them as pioneers. The mood was exciting and I think everyone grasped the significance of what they were part of because along with the excitement, tears were evident throughout the gathering.

I was especially proud when, in the spring of 2009, we dedicated a time capsule loaded with information about the founding of the college. I wrote a letter to be included which described my feelings about what had happened along with predictions as to the future of the institution. The capsule is scheduled to be opened in 2039 and it will be interesting (if I am still around) to see how my predictions do. Huge thanks goes to history teacher Reggie Jayne who put the project together and spearheaded the effort to get items for inclusion.

As described in Chapter 6, a huge payoff resulted when the Selland College of Applied Technology was officially transferred to us July 1, 2009, completing our rapid evolution to a full comprehensive community college. It had been a complicated and involved journey, but when I retired in August

2009, we had accomplished something that some said could not be done.

From August 2007 to August 2009 we had gone from a position of having no money in the bank to a budget of more than $28 million. We went from one employee (me) and no students or programs, to an institution with five distinct and fully functioning departments typical of a mature comprehensive community college:

■ **Academic/transfer courses and programs for credit.** We started with 1,208 students in January and then with 3,618 students in August of 2009. We employed 11 full time and 63 part-time faculty in January and those numbers grew to 22 full time and 120 part-time in August.

■ **Occupational training courses and programs for credit.** When the Selland College transferred to CWI they were serving nearly 1,100 students, and brought over 70 faculty, 17 support staff, and 17 administrative staff. They also brought over 30 programs offering a variety of technical certificates, advanced technical certificates, and associate of applied technology degrees.

■ **Workforce Development/Business Partnerships.** This unit also transferred with the Selland College and is the non-credit, short-term, job related training department crucial to any successful community college. They offer on-campus training in the areas of healthcare, construction/ apprenticeships, manufacturing and trades, business and professional, computers, and emergency services. They also offer customized training (often at the companies they are contracting with), and online classes. When they transferred, they were serving 12,799 students and with those students came five full time and dozens of part-time instructors along with 13 staff members.

■ **Adult Basic Education.** This department oversees basic tutoring, GED preparation and testing, and English as a Second Language. When this unit transferred to CWI with the Selland College, they were serving 4,206 students and had five full-time and more than 90 part-time instructors. They were offering their services throughout the 10 southwest counties of Idaho.

■ **Community Education.** This division provides short-term personal enrichment classes to the general public and we kicked if off in March 2009. It had operated just six months before I left and had already served 241 people with 90 classes and was growing rapidly.

So with all these functions in place, by fall semester of 2009, we employed more than 100 full time and 200-plus part-time instructors with more than 140 staff and professional personnel. We served more than 3,600 credit students and over 17,000 non-credit students.

9 Reflections

After spending 39 years in education, to have had the opportunity to be part of a team doing such important work and to be in a position to leave a real legacy was truly the chance of a lifetime. It was a college administrator's dream come true.

As I transitioned out of the college scene into retirement in the summer of 2009, the Board of Trustees had just gone through a national search and named Dr. Bert Glandon as the next president. We also had contracted with a nationally recognized firm called the California Collegiate Brain Trust to review all we had done and to make recommendations on the best way to move forward. I have full faith that the board and new president will continue to guide the college to incredible accomplishments.

In looking at other start-ups in urban areas such as ours, I am certain that the College of Western Idaho will grow quickly and become the largest institution in the state within a few years and that the school, along with BSU, will become the major engine driving economic development and workforce training throughout the region. I believe that other counties will join the district and that eventually the community college district may even encompass most of Idaho's 10 southwest counties.

As I look back, I often think about the key people who were in the right place at the right time to make all this happen. As I made the rounds speaking to dozens of groups over the two years, it was always interesting to hear people sort of individually take credit for the community college becoming a reality.

The important thing to remember is that the creation of the community college in truth was the result of many, many people *each* of whom contributed an important piece of the puzzle and *each* one should feel enormous pride. At the risk of leaving some people off the list (and I apologize ahead of time for that) I would like to specifically thank certain people, most of whom I worked with and who made a great contribution.

The following list includes several, many of whom were mentioned throughout the book, but I think there is merit in listing them now.

I commend the Nampa Chamber of Commerce then led by M.C. Niland and Georgia Bowman who started the petition drive and got the community college measure on the ballot. Equally supportive were several other Chambers of Commerce throughout the valley. A leader among them was the Boise Metro Chamber with the effort led by Nancy Vannorsdel and Ray Stark. The Chambers from Eagle and Meridian, especially Teri Sackman, also were vocal supporters.

We all owe a huge debt of gratitude to the voters of Ada and Canyon counties who agreed to tax themselves and create a community college district.

Our Board of Trustees did an amazing job of directing the labor, birth, and nurturing of the college; they put in many hours assisting and taking part in the process far beyond what is normally expected of non-paid positions. Jerry Hess was the first chairman of the original board which included Guy Hurlbutt, M.C. Niland, Mark Dunham, and Hatch Barrett. Stan Bastian and Tammy Ray replaced Jerry and Hatch in the first election after the opening of CWI and served with dedication.

We formed a true partnership with Boise State University without which we would not have glued the many pieces together to kick off a working community college in such an amazingly short time. Special thanks go to Bob Kustra who really pushed the need for a community college early and often to large segments of the valley and to Larry Barnhardt who worked tirelessly with key community leaders to help them understand the need, as well, and for positioning the Selland College for inclusion in a community college. Also from BSU, we are grateful to Sona Andrews, Stacy Pearson, Jane Buser, Kevin Satterlee, David O'Neill, Steve Swain, and James McGuire.

We formed another valuable relationship with the College of Southern Idaho who proved to be a great accreditation partner. Jerry Beck, Jeff Fox, and Mike Mason were instrumental in making everything work.

Community support was essential and we received that in a major way from the J.A. and Kathryn Albertson Foundation, specifically from Joe Scott, Tom Wilford, and Lori Fisher, and through them Rand Spiwak. Another valuable supporter was the Micron Corporation, specifically Mike Reynoldson. Community organizations which were instrumental in getting the college approved included the Idaho Association of Commerce and Industry and the Idaho Business Coalition for Education Excellence. Key individuals were Steve Ahrens, Alex LaBeau, Gary Michael, and Kevin Learned.

Governor Butch Otter and then State Senator and now Lieutenant Governor Brad Little were unabashedly vocal in their support from the beginning. Several Ada County legislators were also supportive. The "Community College Yes" campaign was ably led by co-chairs Jerry Hess, Gary Michael, M.C. Niland, and Skip Oppenheimer along with Hatch Barrett, Guy Hurlbutt, Jerry Gunstream, and Skip Smyser as finance co-chairs.

Support from the State Board of Education was crucial. Milford Terrell, Rod Lewis and Mike Rush were especially supportive and deeply involved. Equally as important was the State Division of Professional Technical Education specifically Ann Stephens, Kirk Dennis, and Dick Ledington.

Local political and civic leaders were vocal in their support of the creation of the college. Leading the list were Boise Mayor Dave Bieter, Meridian Mayor Tammy deWeerd, and Nampa Mayor Tom Dale. Canyon County Commissioner Dave Ferdinand also was a strong supporter from the beginning. The valley school superintendents were all CWI backers, but especially out front on the whole issue was Boise Superintendent Stan Olsen, Meridian Superintendent Linda Clark, Nampa Superintendent Gary Larsen, and Caldwell Superintendent Roger Quarles. Civic and professional organizations also stepped up including the Soroptimists of Caldwell, and the Association of Realtors of both Caldwell and Nampa.

We had amazing help from a number of consultants. They included Jerry Gee, Dave Teater, Kathy Hagler, Sally Anderson, and Stephanie Worrell. We simply could not have jump-started the college without their valuable assistance.

Last, but certainly not least, were the people who really did the heavy lifting—my team. Victor Watson brought an incredible background and wealth of experience to us and we simply could not have melded the big concepts without him. He fully understood the whole picture of what was needed to start a college.

Cheryl Wright brought a unique experience base to us with her strong background in both private and public finance and budgeting and was one of the few people who really understood Idaho's professional-technical budgeting system.

Brian Currin brought to us an amazing information technology background and he accomplished the nearly impossible task of tying eight locations, spread across the valley, to a central server with a 21st Century computer system encompassing all the information needed for the college to grow for years to come. He also led the effort to lease and build out several locations.

Shirl Boyce was a unique supporter because he seemed to know everyone in the valley and everyone knew him. He was indispensable in helping me gain access into the community and meet with key groups and individuals and he drove the effort to get our brand new school marketed and established.

Cathy Hampton brought a huge institutional memory to us regarding Boise State University and Selland College and was instrumental in doing so many things including human resources, research, special projects, and practically anything else we needed.

I especially want to thank Debbie Jensen who was my personal assistant for eight years and who is the most dedicated, hard-working, and loyal person with whom I have ever worked. She tackled everything I threw at her and was eager for more.

These six individuals really made the college happen and worked many long (and sometimes frustrating) hours in the process. They never lost hope and I can't thank them enough. I treasure the two years we worked together and will always think of them with fond memories. I count them as lifelong friends.

Together with all these people, and many, many more, we leave a lasting legacy of hope. Hope to the rural student who is struggling but still has a dream; hope to the single parent searching for the best way to support his/her children; hope to the good student who simply can't afford to go directly to a university; hope to anyone who has lost a job and must retrain; hope to the inmate wishing to lead a productive life; hope to an endless list of other people each with their own stories; and last, hope to our struggling economy as more and more businesses are attracted to our area because of a competent and trained workforce.

Victor Watson had a saying that I used often in my presentations, "For some, community college is their first chance, for some it is their only chance, and for some it is their last chance." The citizens of Treasure Valley should take great pride in their vote and support of the College of Western Idaho which has given the entire region hope.

Acknowledgements

This is the part of the book where I have the privilege of thanking the people who directly helped with me with writing this book. I was very fortunate to have so many informed and willing partners in this project. Many thanks:

To the members of my executive team, Dr. Victor Watson, Cheryl Wright, Brian Currin, Shirl Boyce, Cathy Hampton, and Debbie Jensen who were instrumental in helping me remember facts, dates, places, and all the other details that were so important.

To the other College of Western Idaho people who were so helpful. They were Dr. Vera McCrink, Dr. Rick Aman, Brenda Pettinger, Joy Palmer, Grace Barnes, Chris Simon, Terry Blom, Jennifer Couch, Audrey Eldridge, and Reggie Jayne.

Three Board of Trustee members assisted in the very same way. They were M.C. Niland, Guy Hurlbutt, and Mark Dunham. I am very grateful for their time.

To Mike Reynoldson with the Micron Corporation and Jason Lehosit who directed the "Community College Yes" campaign and who provided valuable information concerning the events leading up to and during the campaign. Mike Tracy of Tracy Communications was helpful as well.

To Steve Ahrens, retired President of the Idaho Association of Commerce and Industry, who was very willing to share his comprehensive knowledge regarding the history of the community college movement in Idaho.

To Chris Latter, Communications Officer with the J.A. and Kathryn Albertson Foundation, who really filled in the gaps as to the foundation's rather substantial involvement in the creation of the college.

To Dr. Jerry Gee who was more than willing to share his experience as he helped us navigate the transfer of the Selland College from Boise State, and to Dr. Trudy Anderson who was so helpful in providing information regarding the history of the Selland College.

To Stephanie Worrell who spent time to share her experiences working to get the community college on the public's radar and for helping us get the marketing plan up and running.

And to my talented editor and friend, Larry Gardner, who had the onerous task of sorting through my ramblings and was a great help in refining everything into some sort of coherent document. I appreciate him very much.

Timeline: Creation of the College of Western Idaho

1932 – Boise Junior College is created

1939 – First vocational technical classes start at BJC

1965 – BJC becomes Boise College (junior college mission continues)

1969 – BC becomes Boise State College (junior college mission continues)

1974 – BSC becomes Boise State University (junior college mission continues)

1983 – Idaho Association of Commerce & Industry produces the report entitled *Higher Education in Idaho: A Plan for the Future* calling for a statewide community college system

1984-2003 – Numerous studies conducted regarding need for community college

1988 – BSU creates the College of Technology to include the School of Vocational Technical Education

1997 – BSU creates the Larry G. Selland College of Applied Technology

2004 **February** – BSU President Bob Kustra gives first speech regarding need for a community college

July – Albertson Foundation (JKAF) sets direction to find a way to start a community college

2005 **June** – Governor Kempthorne floats idea of seed money for expansion of community colleges/JKAF makes inquiry of Treasure Valley Community College about interest in expanding/JKAF receives first proposal from BSU

October – BSU presents second proposal to JKAF/JKAF asks Treasure Valley Community College for a proposal

2006 **January** – Governor Kempthorne proposes plan for $5 million seed money for community colleges/Two legislators offer plan for statewide community college system

March – JKAF offers $15 million to State Board of Education to start a community college

April –A legislative Community College Interim Subcommittee studies issue for the summer

June – JKAF meets with Idaho Business Coalition for Education Excellence, Idaho Association of Commerce and Industry, and the Chamber of Commerce along with city and county officials and associations

October – JKAF launches the "Community College Now" campaign

2007 **January** – Governor Otter proposes $5 million seed money for any local district starting a community college in his state of the state address

February – Nampa Chamber of Commerce starts petition drive to put the community college issue on the ballot

March – "Community College Yes" campaign is launched/State Board of Education approves petition to put to a vote creating a community college district

May – The referendum is held and passed creating the community college/JKAF announces a pledge of $10 million for CWI

July – State Board selects Jerry Hess, M.C. Niland, Mark Dunham, Hatch Barrett, and Guy Hurlbutt as the first Board of Trustees for CWI

August – Board of Trustees appoints Dr. Dennis Griffin as the first president.

September –President Griffin selects Dr. Victor Watson, Cheryl Wright, Brian Currin, Shirl Boyce, Cathy Hampton, and Debbie Jensen to serve on the Executive Team

December – Agreement signed to designate CWI as the professional technical training provider for Region III of Idaho

2008 **January** – Non-credit classes start under CWI in a contractual agreement with BSU/President Griffin testifies before the Joint Finance & Appropriations Committee along with both the Senate and House Education Committees

February – Initial approval given by the State Board of Education for the transfer of Boise State's West Campus and the Canyon County Center to CWI

July – Accreditation partnership agreement signed with the College of Southern Idaho

September – Partnership with CSI approved by the Northwest Commissions on Colleges and Universities

October – Moved administrative offices to Aspen Creek Building

November – Elections are held and two new Board of Trustee members are elected/Strategic Plan approved by Trustees

December – Stan Bastian and Tammy Ray sworn in as new Trustees replacing Jerry Hess and Hatch Barrett

All of 2008 – Done simultaneously

-Development of 2008 & 2009 budget/Development of business plan/Development of a branding and marketing plan/Memorandums of Understanding signed to create partnerships with Boise State University, College of Southern Idaho, several consultants, and others/Development of employee and student policies and procedures/Created systems and operational procedures/Developed a strategic plan/Researched, purchased and implemented new operational computer system/Numerous, ongoing negotiations for several properties/Regular meetings to plan the transfer of the Selland College from BSU/Researched and negotiated an employee benefits package/Hired MIG Corporation to create a campus master plan/and the constant hiring and training of new employees

2009 **January** – College grand opening/First credit classes start/President Griffin testifies for second time before State Legislative committees

April – Agreement reached with the Sundance Corporation to lease facility for the creation of the Ada County Center

July – Formal transfer of BSU's Selland College to CWI/Application for Consideration of Candidacy for Accreditation process initiated/California Collegiate Brain Trust is hired to conduct a review of progress of college/Dr. Berton Glanden starts as next president

August – Full Comprehensive college in place/Start of credit students begins

Abbreviations and Acronyms

AS – Associate of Science Degree

AAS – Associate of Applied Science Degree

BSU – Boise State University

CSI – College of Southern Idaho

CWI – College of Western Idaho

ERP – Enterprise Resource Planning Computer System

IACI – Idaho Association of Commerce and Industry

JKAF – J.A. and Kathryn Albertson Foundation

LSCAT – Larry G. Selland College of Applied Technology

NWCCU – Northwest Commission of Colleges and Universities

ORP – Optional Retirement Program

PERSI – Public Employees Retirement System of Idaho

PTE – Professional Technical Education

RN – Registered Nurse

SBOE – State Board of Education

SDPTE – State Division of Professional Technical Education

TVCC – Treasure Valley Community College

About The Author

Dennis Griffin was born and raised in Payette, Idaho. He holds three college degrees, receiving a doctorate from the University of Idaho in 1996. He has a varied work history, and among other things, spent an early career in banking but soon knew that education would be the endeavor that excited him most.

After receiving his bachelor's degree from Boise State College in 1970, he spent the next 10 years teaching in two different high schools during which time he earned a masters degree in counseling from the College of Idaho in 1974. He left high school teaching and moved to private post-secondary professional technical education serving as a Director of Education, School Director, and President/CEO of a company owning several schools. He served in these roles both in Boise and in Seattle.

He returned to public education when he started with Boise State University in 1989 serving as a Division Manager in the professional technical department and then as the Executive Director of the West Campus for the university. He served in these capacities for 18 years. He was named President of the newly formed College of Western Idaho in 2007.

He was deeply involved in the community spending time on numerous boards and advisory councils. While in Seattle, he served as President of the Washington Federation of Private Vocational Schools and, as President of the Pacific Northwest Business Schools Association, was active in the Seattle

Chamber of Commerce. After returning to Boise, he became involved in numerous civic organizations including the Nampa Rotary Club serving as President in 2002-03. He was named Chairman of the Board for the Nampa Chamber of Commerce in 1998-99 and was a member of the Caldwell Chamber of Commerce Board of Directors as well. He also became active in such professional organizations as the Idaho Lifelong Learning Association and served on the Executive Committee of the National Association of Branch Campus Administrators.

After spending thirty-two years in the National Guard and Army Reserve, he retired as a Lieutenant Colonel. He is married to his wife Joni and has three grown children, Scott, Christine, and Jennifer and two grandchildren, Ella and Erika.

RIDENBAUGH
PRESS

Made in the USA
Charleston, SC
12 December 2011